COMMEMORATING CANADA:
HISTORY, HERITAGE, AND MEMORY, 1850s–1990s

Commemorating Canada is a concise narrative overview of the development of history and commemoration in Canada, designed for use in courses on public history, historical memory, heritage preservation, and related areas.

Examining why, when, where, and for whom historical narratives have been important, Cecilia Morgan describes the growth of historical pageantry, popular history, textbooks, historical societies, museums, and monuments through the nineteenth and twentieth centuries. Showing how Canadians have clashed over conflicting interpretations of history and how they have come together to create shared histories, she demonstrates the importance of history in shaping Canadian identity. Though public history in both French and English Canada was written predominantly by white, middle-class men, Morgan also discusses the activism and agency of women, immigrants, and Indigenous peoples. The book concludes with a brief examination of present-day debates over Canada's history and Canadians' continuing interest in their pasts.

(Themes in Canadian History)

CECILIA MORGAN is a professor in the Department of Curriculum, Teaching and Learning at the Ontario Institute for Studies in Education, University of Toronto.

THEMES IN CANADIAN HISTORY

Editor: Colin Coates

CECILIA MORGAN

Commemorating Canada: History, Heritage, and Memory, 1850s–1990s

UNIVERSITY OF TORONTO PRESS
Toronto Buffalo London

© University of Toronto Press 2016
Toronto Buffalo London
www.utppublishing.com
Printed in Canada

ISBN 978-1-4426-4128-0 (cloth)   ISBN 978-1-4426-1061-3 (paper)

♾ Printed on acid-free, 100% post-consumer recycled paper with
vegetable-based inks

Library and Archives Canada Cataloguing in Publication

Morgan, Cecilia, 1958–, author
Commemorating Canada : history, heritage, and memory, 1850s–1990s /
Cecilia Morgan.

(Themes in Canadian history)
Includes bibliographical references and index.
ISBN 978-1-4426-4128-0 (bound)   ISBN 978-1-4426-1061-3 (paperback)

1. Public history – Canada.   2. Memorials – Canada.   3. Collective
memory – Canada.   4. Canada – Anniversaries, etc.   5. Canada –
History – 19th century.   6. Canada – History – 20th century.
7. Canada – Historiography.
I. Title.   II. Series: Themes in Canadian history

FC149.M67 2016   971.04   C2015-907062-7

University of Toronto Press acknowledges the financial assistance to its
publishing program of the Canada Council for the Arts and the Ontario
Arts Council, an agency of the Government of Ontario.

Canada Council   Conseil des Arts
for the Arts   du Canada

ONTARIO ARTS COUNCIL
CONSEIL DES ARTS DE L'ONTARIO
an Ontario government agency
un organisme du gouvernement de l'Ontario

Funded by the   Financé par le
Government   gouvernement
of Canada   du Canada

Canadä

To Laura Dodson and Paul Jenkins

Contents

Acknowledgments

Writing a short book that covers much ground was both demanding and exhilarating. I would like to thank Colin Coates for inviting me to contribute to the Themes in Canadian History series and for his thoughtful suggestions on earlier drafts of the manuscript, all of which made this a much richer study of commemoration and the history of collective memory in Canada. Len Husband and Lisa Jemison of the Press, and Beth McAuley and Melissa MacAulay of The Editing Company, helped see this manuscript through to completion. Thanks, too, to Jerry Bannister for guiding me to material on the history of public memory and commemoration in Newfoundland, and to Melanie Hamilton for her help in locating a wide-ranging body of articles, book chapters, and monographs. The anonymous reviewer of this manuscript offered excellent suggestions; I've attempted, where possible, to incorporate them.

Teaching TPS1427 at the University of Toronto persuaded me that a historically grounded study of commemoration would be useful. As well, lecturing to students in the Willowbank School of Restoration Arts, Queenston, Ontario, showed me where the gaps were in the field and how I might attempt to fill them; this is a much better book because of that experience. Accordingly, then, I would like to dedicate *Commemorating Canada* to the late Laura Dodson (1925–2007), C.M. From the 1970s until her death, Laura played a central role in preserving Niagara-on-the-Lake's history; in particular, she made it possible for the Willowbank School to be founded and to flourish. Laura was both generous and gracious in her support of all those interested in the past; I hope she would have enjoyed this book. *Commemorating Canada* is also dedicated to Paul Jenkins, for always being willing to listen to me and entertain my obsessions with great love and patience.

COMMEMORATING CANADA:
HISTORY, HERITAGE, AND MEMORY, 1850s–1990s

1

Introduction

In the eighteenth-century Haudenosaunee council house, members of the Iroquois Confederacy recite the history of the League of Peace. In 1824, a group of politicians, journalists, and professional men, mostly English-speaking but some French, come together to form the Literary and Historical Society of Quebec. Some thirty years later, African-Canadian men and women who have escaped the horrors of American slavery and made their way to Canada West tell their stories to American abolitionist Benjamin Drew. In the 1870s and again in the early twentieth century, priests, nuns, members of the Roman Catholic Church's hierarchy, and Quebec's political and commercial elite march through the streets of Quebec City to honour the memory of Bishop Laval. In 1884, descendants of Upper Canadian Loyalists remember their ancestors' arrival in the colony with gatherings and monuments. During the 1920s, Nova Scotia's Helen Creighton begins to gather folk tales and songs, while Canadians simultaneously mark Confederation's Diamond Jubilee with historic pageants. Over the course of the twentieth century, the Historic Sites and Monuments Board and Parks Canada put up plaques to particular individuals and events and restore buildings that are deemed "historic." Meanwhile, in schoolrooms across the country, children learn versions of "Canada's story," narratives that often have been generated by these groups and individuals.

Commemorating Canada takes as its subject Canadians' multi-stranded and multifaceted work of crafting historical narratives about their country, region, and locality; it seeks to explore the variety of genres and methods that people have used to establish a relationship with the past. This book tackles a number of themes and addresses certain arguments. For one, it has become an extremely popular lament, often voiced by groups such as the Dominion Institute, media commentators, and certain professors and teachers of history, that Canadians not only do not "know" their own history but that this regrettable historical amnesia has long been a feature of Canadian society, particularly within English Canada. Unlike their counterparts south of the border, Canadians, this argument runs, have not celebrated their past by producing central, founding narratives. Canadians, and perhaps even "Canadian history," have not created those "heroes" – let alone "heroines" – worthy of such attention, who then go on to be memorialized in genres such as monuments, school textbooks, poetry, prose, song, and film. However, rather than telling us much about the state of historical knowledge or awareness in contemporary Canadian society, these claims probably highlight the commentators' present-day situation and anxieties about a number of issues, such as national identity, political, economic, and social change in Canada, and new forms of technology and media. Others have made similar arguments concerning students' historical knowledge in the United States, England, and Scotland, for example. Moreover, fretting about Canadians' historical awareness has its own particular history. Claims that high school students, for example, do not have a good grasp of central dates and important historical actors, or that Canadians do not care much about their "national" past, are not at all new. A number of Canadians, both prominent and less well-known, made similar charges in the nineteenth century.

Placing these discussions in their historical context also leads us to explore the varied and numerous ways that

Canadians have thought about their past and grappled with its meanings. Influenced both by other historical studies and theoretical work, a number of historians have explored the role of the nineteenth- and twentieth-century Canadian state – national, provincial, and municipal – in shaping particular types of narratives and guiding efforts to ensure that such histories be recognized, whether as monuments, plaques, historic sites, museums, or the regulation of history teaching in elementary and secondary school classrooms. The history of commemoration in Canada includes a range of actors who had their own reasons for participating in commemorative activities. Some members of Canadian society were primarily concerned about the histories of their province, region, town, or locality; they might also, though, simultaneously link those histories to that of "Canada." Aboriginal Canadians might insist on their inclusion in the latter while also reminding themselves and non-Aboriginal Canadians that their distinct histories must be remembered. A number of Canadians, whether of British, European, or Asian descent, sought to preserve memories and histories of their ancestral homes; at the same time, many linked those narratives to histories of their experiences in Canada. Women's organizations (often, although not exclusively, composed of middle-class women of British or Anglo-American descent) struggled to ensure that women's contributions to the formation of Canadian society not be forgotten, while also supporting – and sometimes playing a leading role in – commemorations of figures such as Isaac Brock. Members of Canada's labour movement, while often denied access to the leisure and material resources needed to engage in public memory, marked their histories through public demonstrations such as Labour Day parades. While less has been written about African-Canadians' participation in commemoration, the publication of fugitive slave narratives, the formation of Black historical societies in the 1970s and 1980s, and efforts to locate and memorialize the Underground Railroad in southern Ontario, for example, all suggest African-Canadians' persistence in crafting historical narratives.

Moreover, while these groups were concerned about the relationship between their particular histories and that of the Canadian nation and the state, many also believed that family histories and genealogies, narratives of intimate and private life, also had worth and legitimacy as an important repository of historical knowledge. While crafting nineteenth-century genealogies has often been associated with elites, such as the Loyalists of Upper Canada and New Brunswick or upper-middle-class French Canadians, it has also been used by other groups or communities as a way of combating social marginalization. For example, Acadians in nineteenth- and twentieth-century Quebec and the Maritimes sought to establish their genealogical links to groups of ancestors as a way of distinguishing their specific family histories from each other. In this way, they established concepts of their own families, and of themselves, as being distinct and special – or "not ordinary," in the words of one genealogist. Genealogies also might provide an alternative to European-dominated notions of family and community. In northwest Saskatchewan, Metis families historically have used a particular concept of family, *wahkootowin*, that looks at the family not as a nuclear unit but, rather, as a broader set of relationships that emphasizes connections and sets out particular norms of social behaviour that help shape economic decisions within the community. While historians have not always recognized the importance of genealogy in providing a diverse range of groups with a link to the past, such studies point the way for further scholarship in this area. Similar explorations can be made in the realm of photography and other forms of material culture – postcards, tourist souvenirs, calendars, and scrapbooks – which both provide information about the past and, through the range of images and representations they deploy, help shape particular kinds of memory and remembering.

In exploring the range of places and genres in which Canadians have grappled with their histories, we also need to consider why knowledge of such activities is important to our understanding of Canada's history. Why, after all, should we be interested in nineteenth-century efforts to memorialize politicians and generals, let alone lesser-known figures? How does our knowledge of historical commemorators' work deepen or add more complexity to our knowledge of Canadian history? Should historians spend precious time and resources on such questions and not on others? After all, a number of prominent historians, not to mention scholars from fields such as literary studies or cultural anthropology, have expressed concern that our focus on historical representations and social memory risks producing work that is trivial and predictable while, simultaneously, being quite fragmented and isolated from the larger historical context. Such charges need to be taken seriously and the challenges they present considered, not as a reason to abandon the study of commemorative practices, but rather as a means of helping us consider why we choose certain areas of study and what we hope to learn from them.

To be sure, historians' decisions are also to some extent shaped by the society in which they live, not just by debates within their own profession or academic circles. Over the last few decades, Canadian society has participated in a new wave of public interest in "the past," however broadly defined. Historical novels; plays, books, documentaries, and movies about both World Wars; family history and genealogy; even popular culture's recycling of motifs, patterns, and genres from the 1960s to the 1980s in music, clothing, hairstyles, and television: all of these suggest a keen desire by a range of Canadians to engage with multiple aspects of the past and for a range of reasons. Historians are not immune from such developments.

Many ways of studying commemoration and public memory exist and, in such a fluid and open-ended process, new areas that once appeared discrete, perhaps even isolated

from each other, can become connected. In the context of
Canadian history, studying commemorative practices – the
putting up of a statue, or the staging of a historical pageant –
has often been a way of bringing together and integrating
cultural, social, and political history, fields that at times may
appear unconnected. Furthermore, while studying the public
representation of a person or event may not shed much new
light on, for example, Jacques Cartier or the War of 1812,
since commemorative practices often shied away from overt
controversy or the discovery of new knowledge, the processes
that went into crafting the representation in question can
tell us much about the fears, hopes, and desires of the society that did so. Why were particular memories or histories
important at some times and not at others? Why did certain
histories predominate at the expense of others, which were
either suppressed or forgotten? Who participated in public
history and why? As the British historian Raphael Samuel
argues, history has served as an important form of social
knowledge, one that has been shaped in a number of places
and by individuals and groups that may or may not have had
"formal" training in the subject. Even if we do not agree with
their perspectives and uses of history, it is important to ask
when, why, and by whom a society remembers; exploring
these questions enhances our understanding of its particular
social, cultural, political, and intellectual dimensions.

As well as debating the potential and pitfalls of studying
the history of commemoration, historians have discussed
the different types of vocabulary and categories that have
emerged in this area. Historians, anthropologists, cultural geographers, sociologists, and others who work in this
area have used a range of terms to describe and classify
these historical processes and the representations they produced. *Commemorating Canada* uses the terms "commemorations," "public history," and "memory" to try to capture a
range of cultural processes in particular historical contexts;
however, there are other terms and categories that historians have used and that should be acknowledged. French

historian Pierre Nora has been internationally recognized for his work on those "*lieux de mémoire*" – sites of memory – constructed in France. In Nora's three-volume collection of essays, *Realms of Memory*, these include monuments, school history texts, symbols, and institutions such as the French flag and France's national library, the anniversaries of important days in French history (14 July, Bastille Day), famous French men and women (Voltaire, Jean-Jacques Rousseau, Joan of Arc), and national exhibitions. For Nora and his colleagues, these entities evoke a set of civic values that made up the French nation and republic and which draw people together; as sites of memory, they are inextricably tied to the nation and help people imagine their relationship to each other as citizens of France.

Nora's work is underpinned by the conviction that in modern society, memory, as a way of organizing our sense of self and our place in society, no longer exists. For him, memory has been a set of commonly shared customs, rituals, and traditions, ones passed down by generations through oral and physical transmission and thus linked to emotions and sensory dimensions. He also argues that, for memory, the space of the local community was traditionally more important than that of the nation-state or the empire. However, the forces of modernization – urbanization and industrialization, the rise of secularism, and the nation-state – have replaced memory with "history," a form of knowledge that differs from memory by its reliance on written texts, linear chronology, rationality, and logic, and, above all, its insistence that present and past constitute different worlds. "Memory" thus belongs to pre-modern, rural societies in which institutions such as the church, agriculture, and the village or small-scale community dominate, while "history" is the way in which modern, urban, industrial, and secular society gives itself meaning, especially as national entity. Unlike memory's more affective and intensely personal dimensions, history is an intellectual enterprise that is prosaic, analytical, and critical, and, above all, abstract.

Nora's arguments have been both provocative and stimu-
lating; not everyone, though, has accepted them completely. A number of historians have suggested that history and
memory are not entirely separate or dichotomous things.
To be sure, most would agree with Nora that Western society
sees the past as representing difference, in that it is understood as having had different values and different forms of
social, political, and cultural structures and hierarchies. As
well, historians trained within the academy are taught to be
sceptical, analytical, and to deal with larger abstract conceptions to help them organize the detailed information
that they gather in their research. Nevertheless, it seems an
exaggeration to argue that there is no longer memory and
that history has triumphed. For example, while historians
tend to place great value on written documents or material
objects that they decode with the help of other documents
and more abstract narratives, documents may themselves
be based on oral histories, ranging from early colonial texts
to modern court records. As well, Nora's narrative is based
on the French example, which does not entirely "fit" with
the Canadian context. Early colonial Canada had no pre-
existing peasant "memory" that was superseded by written
history: instead, First Nations' oral traditions and memories,
while in certain places disrupted or suppressed by European ideas of history, existed alongside written narratives.
Increasingly, as in the 1997 *Delgamuukw* court decision that
determined an Aboriginal land title in northwestern British Columbia, the state eventually came to see Indigenous
understandings of the past as an accurate and complete
account, no less so than those written records produced by
colonial officials. Furthermore, like their counterparts in
other contexts, Canadian historians have made extensive
use of oral histories as a means of recapturing the histories and memories of those who have often been excluded
from, or only partly represented in, written records: workers, women, immigrants, and African-Canadians, for example. In such cases, the use of individual memories has often

been an important means of reconstituting and affirming the history of a particular group.

As well as Nora's "sites of memory," the idea of "invented traditions," coined by historian Eric Hobsbawm and anthropologist Terence Ranger, has been influential with a number of historians. Used to describe particular forms of public displays that rely on notions of tradition and history, such as Coronation ceremonies in late-nineteenth- and twentieth-century Britain or displays of British imperial power in India, invented traditions are practices and performances that, while ostensibly rooted in centuries-old rituals, are of quite recent vintage. Simultaneously, though, they invoke "history" as a source of legitimacy. For example, the popular conviction that the British monarchy has always been "good" at ceremony and spectacle is, according to historian David Cannadine, one that developed in the late Victorian era. Aware of its mid-century decline in popularity, the monarchy sought to reassert itself through public displays of pomp and majesty that relied on historical practices that seemed medieval but in reality were constructed for those occasions; moreover, these practices relied on "modern" forms of technology and communication to be effective and reach large audiences. "Invented traditions" are also ones asserted by powerful nation-states and elites; they inculcate nationalism and are hegemonic in their intent and effect. To be sure, historians have questioned whether all "traditions" of the nineteenth and twentieth centuries can be seen as products of modernity and, also, whether popular audiences were always taken in or persuaded by such spectacles. Nevertheless, Canadian historians have found it useful, particularly in looking at the crafting of the Loyalist myth in Ontario, to work with some elements of this approach.

"Heritage" is another term used by many groups and institutions, one that has become ubiquitous in both the private and public sectors. While not synonymous with "history," it has a long and complex relationship to that term.

Perhaps what makes "heritage" such a difficult term for
historians is that it has no one, uniform meaning; calling a
building, landscape, collection of artefacts, or beliefs and
values "heritage" can mean a number of things to a number
of audiences.

It can be used by governments, nationalists, and institutions, both sacred and secular, as a means of justifying
particular courses of action (and not others) and uphold-
ing certain political and social values, ones that become
invested with qualities such as stability, integrity, authenticity, and venerability. "Defending our heritage" can be
used to oppose social and political change. The ban on
fox hunting in Britain, for example, or the admission of
formerly excluded groups to positions of authority in universities, has been met with the argument that such actions
attack a cherished "heritage," a way of doing things that is
intrinsically valuable because of its link to the past (albeit
one that is sometimes as much imagined as real). Historians also have pointed to governments' use of "heritage
designation" in promoting the conservation and preservation of certain buildings, sites, and landscapes, measures
which might result in the protection and promotion of
places associated with the history of the rich and powerful to uphold certain types of conservative and nationalist
values in the present. As well, "heritage" can be found in
myriad places in the realm of consumption and advertising, used to describe commodities such as real estate, food
and drink, furniture, and textiles. In this case, sometimes
the connection between the use of heritage and the history
of the object or commodity so designated has been hazy
and at times completely spurious. In these examples, "heritage" can mean the antithesis of "history," as it implies a
past frozen in time, devoid of conflict and complexity, and
reduced to a collection of objects. However, "heritage" has
been taken up by those who, until relatively recently, have
not been well-represented in either historians' accounts or
in the activities of commemorators and those who sought

to shape public understandings of the past. "Heritage" can also refer to the histories and memories of workers, women, First Nations, African-Canadians, and other racial and ethnic groups, all of whom advocate for a broader-based "people's history" that calls for a more inclusive conception of the past and for greater recognition of the distinctive histories of their groups. The Workers' Arts and Heritage Centre in Hamilton, Ontario, for example, explores the histories of a wide-ranging group of workers in Canada and, where possible, internationally; it also promotes the artistic and cultural work of multiple communities in the city and elsewhere.

Commemorating Canada, then, looks at a range of activities in which Canadians have attempted to craft historical narratives: the writing of history in the nineteenth century, the formation of museums and historical societies, the erection of monuments, the commemoration of war, tourism, and the teaching of history in elementary and secondary school classrooms. It does not look at the teaching of history in Canadian universities, a story with its own complexities that has been told elsewhere by scholars such as Carl Berger and Donald Wright. At times, though, I touch upon the relationship between university-based history and that which was taught and enacted outside of academic institutions. Moreover, Commemorating Canada makes no claim to being completely comprehensive in its coverage. Some topics, such as nineteenth- and early-twentieth-century African-Canadians' communities' work in crafting their past, have not yet been explored in great detail by historians. In this and in other instances, I suggest that these are topics that historians might explore further, building on the work from which I have drawn on for this book, but also bringing new insights to our understanding of the importance of history as a form of political, social, and cultural knowledge.

The past has mattered to a range of Canadians because it has been caught up in questions of power and identity. However, those questions can only be understood in their particular contexts, those of place and time. We need to explore when, why, and for whom an understanding of the past has been important. In a similar vein, we also need to consider the consequences of commemorative activities and the creation of historical memory.

2

History and Memory, 1750s–1870s

Although the nineteenth century saw the emergence of history as an academic discipline, as well as a growth in published written texts in British North America (and elsewhere) and a growing public interest in the past, the use of narrative and storytelling to reflect on experiences, both those that occurred within living memory and those of one's ancestors, has, of course, a much longer history. First Nations people within the northern portion of North America used oral histories and various forms of written and material communication, such as pictographs and wampum, to create accounts of their past before contact with non-Indigenous people. They also created narratives to serve moral and didactic purposes, stories that not only told their audiences about people's relationships to the land, to spiritual beings and practices, and to each other, but also taught lessons that reflected First Nations communities' practices and values. These narratives were critically important in educating their children: they told boys and girls about their peoples' histories and helped socialize them into their future roles as members of their communities. After contact with Europeans, in settings such as treaty negotiations or in meetings with royalty and other prominent individuals, Indigenous leaders presented historical accounts of their communities' use of land, water, and other resources and of their social and cultural practices, structures, and values. In these meetings they relied on a variety of methodologies, such as speeches, dress, and types of performance and ritual, to make their points. Moreover, First Nations communities also continued to tell their histories to themselves and to other Indigenous groups. For example, over the course of the eighteenth century, during their council meetings, members of the Six Nations Iroquois recited narratives that told of the benefits of their historic alliances, both with each other and with Europeans.

Indigenous people also adapted European literary practices for their own purposes and uses and wrote down their histories in letters, petitions, and book-length manuscripts. In the mid-eighteenth century, a Mohawk man known as "David of Schoharie" wrote down the trials endured by his people with the coming of Europeans and the need for long-standing traditions and practices to be maintained. Transcribed from a copy at the Six Nations reserve in Upper Canada, his text was translated into English in the 1830s and published later in the century by anthropologist Horatio Hale as *The Iroquois Book of Rites*. As well, in the mid-nineteenth century, the Anishinabe (Ojibwa) Methodist missionaries and writers Kahkewaquonaby (Peter Jones) and Kahgegagabowh (George Copway) penned histories of their people. Kahkewaquonaby's *History of the Ojibway Indians*, written in the early 1840s and published posthumously in 1861 through the efforts of his English wife, Eliza Field, covered a wide range of topics and chronology. Kahkewaquonaby used a variety of sources and perspectives in his work, the former including both European travel narratives published in the 1760s and 1770s as well as his own memories of spiritual, social, and political values and practices within his community. Although as a missionary to the Ojibwa he believed in the need for their conversion to Christianity, Kahkewaquonaby also decried their treatment by colonial authorities and settlers, citing their exposure to alcohol, disease, and whites' immoral behaviour towards them as a sad and regrettable chapter in their history. He also castigated Europeans' dispossession of the Ojibwa from their land and resources, done "for a trifling remuneration." Kahgegagabowh's 1850 *Traditional History and Characteristic Sketches of the Ojibwa Nation* used the approach and structure of early ethnographic studies, which posed questions about history, tribal structures, language, government, values and manners, religious beliefs, and daily life. Like Kahkewaquonaby's history, Kahgegagabowh's narrative also pointed to similarities between Ojibwa and settler society in areas such as religion, political organization, and certain economic practices. He also used oral tradition as sources of information, attempting to develop a means of verifying these narratives and transcribing them into a short-story format, one that would become very commonly known as "Indian legends." Kahgegagabowh's and Kahkewaquonaby's histories, along with that written by Minnesota Ojibwa William Warren, also provided valuable accounts of Iroquois-Ojibwa relations in the Great Lakes.

Little has been written by historians of commemoration and public memory about African-Canadians in the late eighteenth and nineteenth centuries. Nevertheless, African-Canadians narrated their histories in a number of places, such as slave narratives, histories, and memoirs. John Marrant, for example, published his history, *Narrative of the Lord's Wonderful Dealings with John Marrant, a Black (Now Going to Preach the Gospel in Nova Scotia)*, in 1785 in London. Writing one's history could also be done in the petition, a means of addressing the government used by a number of colonists from a range of backgrounds. In 1821, Loyalist soldier Richard Pierpoint petitioned the Upper Canadian government in a bid to gain passage back to Africa. In attempting to make his case, Pierpoint crafted a narrative of his personal history, one bound up with the transatlantic slave trade, the American Revolution, and the War of 1812. "'Your Excellency's Petitioner,' Pierpoint wrote, 'is a Native of Bondon in Africa ... at the age of sixteen years he was made a prisoner and sold as a slave ... he was conveyed to America about the year 1769; and sold to a British officer; ... he served his Majesty during the American Revolutionary War in the Corps called Butler's Rangers; and again during the late American War in a Corps of Color raised on the Niagara Frontier.'"[1] (Pierpoint, unfortunately, was unsuccessful in his attempt to return to his birthplace and died in the colony's Garafraxa Township.)

Fugitive slave narratives, in which African-Canadians narrated their escape from American slavery through the Underground Railroad, also contributed to their communities' public history; one such example was Thomas Smallwood's narrative, published in 1851 in Toronto. Although the primary purpose of the published narratives was to illustrate the horrors of slavery in the American South and contrast it with the freedom offered by Canada, the narratives themselves are full of details about individual, family, and community histories, both in the United States and in Canada West. Furthermore, in the nineteenth and twentieth centuries, African–Nova Scotian churches created valuable histories of local communities by putting together commemorative volumes that celebrated the churches' founding and marked particular milestones. As well, over the course of the nineteenth century, African-Canadians in southern Ontario and the Niagara area came together to celebrate the anniversary of Emancipation Day, 1 August 1834, which marked the end of slavery in the British Empire.

After the First World War, University of Western Ontario historian Fred Landon began collecting research materials on the history of the abolitionist movement and Underground Railroad, and started to present his findings to the Ontario Historical Society in the 1920s. Landon's research has been seen as an important, path-breaking step in the development of African-Canadian history, one all

---

1 Cited in Michael Power and Nancy Butler, *Slavery and Freedom in Niagara* (Niagara-on-the-Lake, ON: Niagara Historical Society, 2000), 45.

the more striking because it appeared in both academic and public history circles. Historical societies, monuments, publications, and museum exhibitions dedicated to the preservation and public display of African-Canadian history emerged in the twentieth century, particularly in the post–Second World War decades.

Indigenous and African-Canadian histories tended to focus on their respective communities' survival and persistence in the face of dislocation and upheaval. However, with some exceptions, their narratives tended to receive less attention than other histories created during this period. From the mid-eighteenth century on, colonists of British, Anglo-American, and European origin engaged in highly visible and publicly debated attempts to create a "past" for British North America, both within its boundaries and across the ocean. Promoters of emigration, journalists, lawyers, and political leaders sought to write histories of the Maritime colonies, Lower and Upper Canada, the Pacific Northwest Coast, and Vancouver Island that served a range of purposes. "Promoters" of the Maritimes hoped to attract emigrants by providing descriptions of the geographic, political, and social conditions of their respective colonies. The first known piece of writing along these lines was an anonymous pamphlet entitled *A Geographical History of Nova Scotia*. Published in 1749 in London, *A Geographical History* provided a long list of the colony's topography, climate, and soils; it also, though, included an account of British and French struggles for its control. Over the following decade, other writers, some based in London, others resident in the Maritimes, produced accounts of Nova Scotia that told readers of the triumph of the British military might over the French and suggested that perceived dangers, such as Acadians and Indigenous people, had now been subdued; the province was thus safe for prospective settlers. In 1806, Scottish-born John Stewart, a resident of Prince Edward Island, published a history of his new home that sought to mend fences between the Island's opposing factions and to repair its reputation in Britain, which had been damaged by strife between certain Island residents and absentee landlords.

History, then, could be used in a number of ways. By providing narratives of bloody and complicated conflicts which glossed over existing tensions and pointed to the triumph of British institutions and values, attempted to unite opposing groups within colonial society, and reassured the British population that Nova Scotia and Prince Edward Island were now safe places, these writers not only chronicled the past according to their own needs and desires, but they also attempted to ensure a future marked by optimism and progress. With the publication of Thomas C. Haliburton's two-volume *An Historical and Statistical Account of Nova Scotia* in 1829, such promotional texts were written by those born and raised in the Maritime colonies, people who saw themselves as patriots as well as promoters. Their accounts of Nova Scotia, New Brunswick, and Prince Edward Island attributed progress to the presence of a group of "yeomen" farmers, men whose independence and resilience had laid the foundation for colonial prosperity. These accounts did little to acknowledge internal cleavages within colonial society of religion, class, race, or ethnicity. They did, though, fulfil their authors' desire to create useful histories that would provide outside audiences with a portrait of united and homogenous societies.

Historians of the Canadas also had their own political and social reasons for writing histories of the colonies. In 1744, Pierre-François-Xavier de Charlevoix, a teacher, missionary, and explorer, wrote his history of New France as a record of Catholic missionaries' work among Aboriginal people. Although Charlevoix wished to ensure that the missionaries' devotion to their work was entered into the historical record, his was not just a hagiographic account. Charlevoix used written documents, oral tradition wherever possible, and secondary sources; he also criticized the government of New France for its perceived shortcomings (greed, corruption, and neglect). The conquest of New France in 1759–60 stalled, it would seem, the writing of the colony's history by French historians. Those anglophone historians who followed Charlevoix – George Heriot, William Smith, and John Fleming – were, perhaps not surprisingly, interested in demonstrating that the history of New France was one of neglect by the French government, arbitrary and despotic abuse by local governors, and economic stagnation. The arrival of British rule was close to an act of divine intervention, as it brought political liberty and commercial progress. French Canadians might – and, as we shall see, did – dispute such claims, although some French-Canadian clerical historians agreed that the British conquest was providential as it allowed French Canada to avoid the excesses of the French Revolution. Nevertheless, the anglophone interpretation of New France's history proved to be widely influential with English-speaking Canada well into the nineteenth century. Such an interpretation was also bolstered by American writer Francis Parkman, whose histories had a very significant effect on both American and English-speaking Canadian historians' understanding of New France, one that lasted well into the twentieth century. Parkman's epic histories of the colony, full of literary embellishments and flourishes, depicted the contest between Britain and France for its possession as a moral struggle in which Britain emerged the victor. Because of a tyrannical government and a domineering church, New France's society was doomed; all of its structures, practices, and values were inadequate (although later historians would argue about which of them was the most detrimental) and it was destined by divine Providence to fail.

Histories of Upper Canada, for their part, were no less influenced by political ideas and by the colony's political life. Since the colony was created much later than New France and Nova Scotia, initial writing about it in the late eighteenth century focused on its physical characteristics and its future prospects, and less so its history. The history of those First Nations resident in Upper Canada before white settlement played little, if any, role in such work. When histories began to be written in the decades after the War of 1812, they were shaped by their authors' positions on matters of political reform and the colony's future. One of the best-known works, Scottish-born Robert Gourlay's 1822 two-volume *A Statistical Account of Upper Canada, Compiled with a View to a Grand System of Emigration*, stressed the history and significance of loyalty and patriotism, qualities that had supposedly been brought to the colony from Britain and that made it an outpost of British civilization in a frontier "wilderness" (in fact, Gourlay's history was based on Scotland's *Statistical Accounts*). Gourlay's writings also invoked the notion of patriotic reform. Arguing that the colony's loyal patriots needed to maintain constant vigilance of their government to ensure that British values were upheld, Gourlay insisted that dissent and a critical stance towards the state were an important part of Upper Canada's past, present, and future. In the 1820s and 1830s, Gourlay himself figured as a historical actor in public narratives of the colony's history. For example, reform politician William Lyon Mackenzie attacked the colony's elite, the "Family Compact," for having suppressed patriotism by imprisoning, trying, and banishing Gourlay, and for their treatment of a number of other reformers in the early 1800s. In 1862, Mackenzie's son-in-law, Charles Lindsey, reiterated this narrative with the publication of his two-volume biography, *The Life and Times of Wm. Lyon Mackenzie*. Lindsey's book also included an account of the 1837 Rebellion in Upper Canada. Mackenzie's construction of the colony's political history was not the sole account, though. In contrast to his focus on the Compact and their historical misdeeds, reformer Robert Baldwin saw the history of Upper Canada as an extension of Britain's past. Upper Canadians, Baldwin believed, were transplanted loyal British subjects who wished to have the same historical safeguards of their liberties and rights as in their "homeland." Accordingly, Baldwin demanded the implementation of the British constitution in Upper Canada as a way of ensuring that British "traditions" would be maintained.

In the Pacific Northwest, most accounts that dealt with the region's past began to appear in the 1840s, sparked by disputes between Britain and the United States over the international boundary. Both sides wished to prove that they had been first to explore and occupy the territory. American writers asserted a history of American explorers, fur traders, and settlers, one in which Britain had no historical presence and therefore no claim to the area. If Britain's presence was acknowledged, it was because of the Hudson's Bay Company (HBC), an organization that these writers saw as antidemocratic and an agent of British imperialism. Indigenous people fared even worse, as they were seen either as violent and treacherous towards the settlers, or simply as vanishing and therefore inconsequential to the area's past, present, and future. British accounts, written to dispute the American versions, focused on explorers such as Francis Drake, James Cook, and George Vancouver; they also tended to praise the activities of the HBC as benevolent and aimed at improving the welfare of First Nations people. In their attempts to demonstrate British imperial superiority, these writers depicted British interactions with Indigenous people as having been motivated by concerns for their well-being, unlike American policies of removal and extermination. Such accounts paid greater attention to First Nations people and did not depict them as negatively as did the American histories. Nevertheless, they tended to ignore Indigenous people as historical actors with their own motivations and concerns and treated them as wards of the Crown and the HBC; their main purpose in these narratives was to demonstrate British moral superiority.

After the 1846 Oregon Treaty, histories of the Northwest were shaped by the British imperial desire to acquire scientific and geographic knowledge of the region. The London-based Royal Geographical Society (RGS) promoted such endeavours, sponsoring (e.g.) a transcontinental railroad line and the Palliser Expedition, which surveyed the Prairies and the Rocky Mountains. Inspired by the Society's work, in 1858 William Hazlitt, a clerk based in the British War Office who would go on to become an esteemed historian, published *British Columbia and Vancouver Island: A Historical Sketch of the British Settlements in the North-West Coast of America*. The first account to use "British Columbia," the name of the just-created colony, in its title, Hazlitt's book was based on earlier histories, RGS records, government documents, and newspaper accounts. Perhaps not surprisingly, British exploration took centre stage, as did the history of the HBC. Hazlitt also spent time discussing Aboriginal people, who, he felt, were not doomed to extinction; rather, if properly converted to Christianity and civilization, they were quite capable of adapting to a changing environment. While Hazlitt's was a scholarly narrative, like writers in the Maritimes or Upper Canada he too was concerned with promoting emigration from Britain to the colony. Hazlitt's work was followed by accounts published in London by naval officers, missionaries, and settlers who arrived in the colony in the late 1850s and 1860s. The most reliable and balanced of the period's histories was Reverend Matthew Macfie's 1865 *Vancouver Island and British Columbia* (Macfie had been a minister in the colonies for five years and toured other British North American colonies and Britain on speaking tours, aimed at attracting settlers to the Northwest). Although he criticized the HBC and James Douglas's colonial government, Macfie believed that the colonies' resources, climate, and hoped-for transcontinental railroad should make it an attractive spot, the "England of the Pacific."

Whatever their specific motivation – promoting emigration, imagining a future, addressing present political wrongs, or laying claim to territory – the authors of these histories shared a tendency to treat their subjects as the past, present, and future of specific and very distinct colonies. For these writers, it was only their ties to Britain that provided a unifying theme that linked their histories to each other. It was not until the 1839 publication of *Lord Durham's Report* that a common history for Nova Scotia, Prince Edward Island, New Brunswick, and Upper and Lower Canada began to emerge. Although we might question Governor Durham's assumptions that these colonies were a unified entity, his treatment of their histories as being a shared story was nonetheless original and would prove influential in the development of national narratives. He believed that shared forms of government, institutions, beliefs, habits, and the struggle for responsible government resulted in a common, not fragmented, history. Moreover, writing colonial histories in such a manner meant distorting them, as Durham tended to see the history of British North America as being that of Upper Canada. Lower Canadian history up to 1763 was a tale of a quasi-feudal society dominated by the military and the Catholic Church. The British government did not improve matters by pampering of the French-speaking population, first by trying to keep them loyal during the American Revolution, then by granting them an assembly in which they would dominate numerically and their own province. The French-Canadian elite, Durham argued, then abused British benevolence by turning the uneducated Lower Canadian peasantry against the Crown in 1837 and by blocking the passage of progressive legislation. "History," for Durham, demonstrated the need for French Canadians' assimilation into English social and political norms.

Durham, Mackenzie, and their contemporaries were not the only ones to assign weight and meaning to the colonial past. The oldest historical society in Canada, the Literary and Historical Society of Quebec (LHSQ), was founded in Quebec City in 1824 under the direction of the Earl of Dalhousie, Canada's governor general. Formally bilingual but dominated by English speakers, the Society's founders wished to preserve, care for, and disseminate the historical records of the colony; it also ran a museum and reference library. The Society was quite successful in meeting its goals. By its 100th anniversary, it had published thirty-five volumes of its series of *Transactions*, which included essays on early Canadian history as well as primary documents. The LHSQ also sponsored lectures on historical and scientific subjects; as well, it played an important role in the establishment of other scholarly societies and organizations, such as the Geological Survey of Canada, Library and Archives Canada, and the Historic Sites and Monuments Board. It was not the only public forum, though, organized to explore Canadian history. Shortly before he died in 1831, the journalist, reform politician, and physician Jacques Labrie requested that his colleague Augustin-Norbert Morin (a fellow Assembly member and writer for the *Patriote* party) complete a history of Canada, a project that Labrie regarded as his final achievement. Labrie had been a critic of Governor Dalhousie, whose administration he regarded as violating the British constitution, and with fellow reformers had organized an 1828 petition to London on that topic. He was also an advocate for education and the medical profession in the colony; in his capacity as a teacher in his parish of Saint-Eustache, Labrie had written manuals on geography and history. Consisting of at least three volumes, each numbering 500 pages, Labrie's history covered the sixteenth century up to the War of 1812. It would have represented a singular achievement, since at the time the only major history of New France was Charlevoix's, which ended in 1733. Unfortunately, political wrangling prevented the manuscript from being published and the only draft was burnt in a house fire in 1837 during the Rebellion.

While the loss of Labrie's history was regrettable, Labrie's interest in the past was shared by a number of Lower Canadians in the years after the Rebellion. The upheavals experienced by the colony (and then province) – political restructuring, the spread of industrialization, the arrival of around 400,000 British immigrants, and urban growth – resulted in a search for solutions to contemporary social and cultural problems. History, it appeared to a number of French Canadians, might hold the answer to such challenges. Simultaneously, the past also might serve as a kind of refuge from a present that was undergoing rapid, and not always welcome, change (a use of the past that was not confined to French Canada). From the 1840s to the 1860s, French-Canadian writers turned their attention to history as a genre in which questions of ethnic and, ultimately, "national" identity could be explored.

The notary, poet, and historian François-Xavier Garneau was perhaps the best-known of these writers. Garneau was well-travelled, having made two trips across the Atlantic in the early 1830s to England and France, where he cultivated his interests in political reform, literature, and history. The 1841 union of the Canadas confirmed Garneau's desire to be a historian, as he felt that French Canada's future survival was dependent on its being able to lay claim to its past. Through his membership in the LHSQ and his work as the French translator to the Legislative Assembly, Garneau was able to begin work on, first, the voyages of Jacques Cartier and, ultimately, his major project, *Histoire du Canada*. Garneau's three-volume history appeared between 1845 and 1848, with supplementary material published in 1853. His work was wide-ranging, to say the least. *Histoire du Canada* opened with the development of Western historical criticism in the Renaissance and documented the history of New France and Lower Canada until 1840. In writing and editing his history, Garneau used material from a number of archives in Quebec City and Albany, New York (the latter held copies of material held in the French national archives), the correspondence of Quebec's English governors up to Dalhousie, and the work of the journalist and historian of Lower Canada Robert Christie. In 1854 and 1855, Garneau also published newspaper accounts of his overseas travels, which were brought together in an 1855 volume, *Voyage en Angleterre et en France dans les années 1831, 1832, et 1833.*

Although it had its critics, Garneau's *Histoire* was generally received very enthusiastically during his lifetime and well after his death. In 1867, a year after Garneau died, a committee was struck to memorialize him by helping his family raise a memorial to him in the Belmont cemetery on the heights of Sainte-Foy; in the early twentieth century, his grandson, Hector Garneau, published an updated version in Paris. On the 100th anniversary of the first edition's publication, a number of ceremonies were held in Montreal, Quebec, and Ottawa to honour Garneau and his work; by 1946, the *Histoire* had gone through eight printings. Today a number of sites in French Canada – lakes, streets, parks, a township, schools, and a college – bear Garneau's name.

Garneau has been seen as nineteenth-century French Canada's "national historian," but he was certainly not alone. Scholars such as abbé Etienne-Michel Faillon, Joseph Doutre, Georges Boucher de Boucherville, and Phillipe Aubert de Gaspé also explored French-Canadian history during this period. Between 1861 and 1865, abbé Jean-Baptiste-Antoine Ferland, a professor at Université Laval (where, among his other duties, he gave public lectures on the history of Canada) published *Cours d'histoire du Canada*, which was, in many respects, a clerical response to Garneau's focus on the state and political developments. Ferland's *Cours* placed the Catholic Church at the centre of colonial society, presenting a portrait of a clerical leadership that coexisted with the civil authority, exemplified values of piety and morality that were followed by the laity, and successfully converted willing and compliant Aboriginal people to Christianity. However, Ferland also was capable of seeing Indigenous behaviour not as mindless savagery (which was often the way that other historians interpreted it) but rather as an expression of their own social values. He also condemned French officials' behaviour towards them, such as Jacques Cartier's kidnapping of the Iroquoians Domagaya and Taignoagny.

As well as writing narratives of the French in New France and Lower Canada, the historians of mid-nineteenth-century Quebec also displayed a keen interest in genealogy, the study of ancestors. At the same time that Ferland's volumes were being published, so too were family histories, such as François Daniel's *Histoire des grandes familles françaises du Canada* (1867) or Cyprien Tanguay's seven-volume *Dictionnaire généalogique des familles canadiennes depuis la fondation de la colonie jusqu'à nos jours* (1871). This quest for forefathers (and sometimes, albeit more rarely, foremothers) took on a particular meaning in the context of nineteenth-century Catholic nationalists. For them, the family was the backbone of the nation; demonstrating deep and continuous family roots would prove that the Quebec nation was itself a historical artefact. Genealogies and family trees would also prove important in other forms of commemoration.

In addition to written histories, genealogies, and family trees, one of the best-known forms, and in many ways longest-lasting forms, of public commemoration in Quebec was coined near the end of this period: the provincial motto. In 1883, the province adopted "*Je me souviens*"; it became part of its coat-of-arms in 1939 and, in 1976, began to be used on license plates. Eugène-Étienne Taché, the architect responsible for the provincial legislature, also suggested the saying. What exactly is to be remembered is, though, a matter of debate. Some French Canadians saw it as the first line of a poem that describes their allegiances to both France and Great Britain, a memory of being born under both "the lily" (the French symbol) and flourishing under "the rose" (the English symbol). Others interpret it as reflecting Taché's own concept of Quebec's distinct history within Confederation (Taché designed the legislature as a pantheon that honoured Quebec's historic figures), while yet another group of Québécois now interpret "*Je me souviens*" as a reminder of historic injustices and wrongs committed by English Canada.

Some of the historians discussed above, such as Ferland, held positions within the growing circle of universities in Quebec, while others resembled Garneau in their professional orientation, being journalists, publishers, lawyers, or newspaper editors. The texts these men wrote – and the vast majority, if not all, were men – reached a growing audience of readers literate in both English and French. An increase in the number of children enrolled in school during the 1840s, the expansion of the province's universities and teacher-training colleges during the mid-nineteenth century, and the development of more societies and institutions devoted to literary and scientific pursuits provided a wider audience for historical narratives. In the late 1830s, this audience was primarily middle-class and urban, since in 1837 the urban literacy rate was 66 per cent and that of rural Quebec was 22 per cent. However, when the 1861 census was taken, it showed a clear increase in literacy in both urban and rural Quebec: the former had risen to 82 per cent, while the latter had gone up to 62 per cent. To be sure, such numbers must be interpreted with caution, not least because census takers often held differing interpretations of literacy. Nevertheless, these figures suggest the creation of an audience of readers over the course of the nineteenth century, who helped support libraries, literary societies, and Mechanics' Institutes.

Such societies and institutions developed somewhat later in British Columbia; however, in the 1870s, the province's history drew the attention of an American publisher, Hubert Howe Bancroft. Originally based in San Francisco, Bancroft moved to the colony in the 1860s. His earlier publications consisted of handbooks that, although generally focused on American locations on the Pacific Coast, also included information about British Columbia. His imagination captured by the possibility of writing a history of North America's western coast, Bancroft established a large-scale oral history project dedicated to the reminiscences of gold-rush pioneers and other settlers, both in British Columbia and in the American Northwest; in Victoria, he also drew upon colonial government records and HBC papers. The result was the two-volume *History of the Northwest Coast* (1884 and 1890) and *History of British Columbia 1792–1887* (1887 and 1890). In these books, Bancroft was less interested in promoting the province to prospective settlers than in capturing a past marked by the pioneers' virtue, a quality symbolized by their bringing civilization to the so-called "wilderness"; the history of British Columbia was the history of Western civilization's triumph on the Pacific Coast. However, although Bancroft admired the British for dealing with Indigenous people more humanely than his American compatriots had done, he saw the British as being motivated not by superior morality, but rather by pragmatism and the pursuit of profit. While Bancroft generally depicted Indigenous people as passive, he admitted that they had contributed to the colony's economy and suggested that they possessed claims, ones based on natural rights, to the Northwest Coast; in both of these stances, Bancroft differed from other contemporary historians of the area. Bancroft also included British Columbia's Chinese residents in his work, discussing their work as gold miners and the history of Victoria's Chinese community. Given the growing strength of anti-Chinese attitudes during the late nineteenth century, his inclusion of the latter group is notable.

In the early 1890s, a number of new arrivals in the province also saw history as playing an important role, one that might bring cohesion and a sense of continuity to a heterogeneous and fluid society. Inspired by the rise of historical societies in their home provinces, John Kerr, Oliver Cogswell, and Alexander Begg had backgrounds in journalism, publishing, and teaching. In Winnipeg, Begg had helped publish the reports of the Historical and Scientific Society of Manitoba (1879–) and had written guidebooks and a historical novel, *"Dot it Down"* (1871), set during the Red River Resistance. These newcomers set out to provide narratives of local history that emphasized national pride and loyalty to Britain. Unlike Bancroft, whose *History of the Northwest Coast* had seen British Columbia as part of a Pacific region, these historians focused on the British explorers and fur traders. For these writers, the HBC had played an important part in fostering the imperial tie, as did the Canadian Pacific Railway. Indigenous people had few, if any, roles in these narratives and Chinese people were mentioned only in the context of the need for their exclusion; "pioneers" of British descent were responsible for the province's strengths and virtues. While limited in their scope and hampered by a lack of archival collections, these histories were not without influence. Cogswell's 1893 *History of British Columbia* was bought by the provincial government for its schools, while Begg was given over $1,000 by the legislature to research, write, and publish his history of the province.

Along with those texts deemed "serious" scholarly works, another form of historical narrative in the nineteenth century was the historical novel. Sir Walter Scott's historical romances of medieval and eighteenth-century Scotland, for example, proved very popular with the English-Canadian reading public, who not only bought his books but, for those who could travel overseas, also visited his home of Abbotsford in Scotland. Scott's example was taken up in Canada during the nineteenth century as a number of writers turned to the genre of historical fiction. Niagara-born John Richardson, a major in the British army who had served in the War of 1812, Europe, and the West Indies, published a number of historical novels: 1832's *Wacousta,* a story of the Odawa chief Pontiac's 1763 uprising on the Detroit frontier and, in 1840, *The Canadian Brothers; or, the Prophecy Fulfilled,* which explored the War of 1812 from a Canadian perspective. Other writers addressed eighteenth-century colonial history through the genre of historical romance. Eliza Lanesford Foster, for example, originally from Massachusetts, wrote historical romances of the American Revolution (*Saratoga* and *Yorktown*) before moving to Montreal in 1840 with her husband, Dr. Frederick Cushing.

Between 1838 and 1851, she wrote short stories, poetry, and historical romances for the magazine *Literary Garland of Montreal* (she also became its editor), as well as articles for magazines in the United States. The best-known female Canadian historical novelist, though, was Rosanna Eleanora Mullins Leprohon. Born in Montreal in 1829, educated at the Congregation of Notre-Dame convent, and married to Jean-Lucien Leprohon (also a doctor), Rosanna Leprohon first wrote poetry inspired by religious, domestic, and Canadian themes, as well as a small number of poems which featured Aboriginal Canadians. Her work, as well as Richardson's, also appeared in the *Literary Garland*. Published between 1859 and 1868, Leprohon's historical novels dealt primarily with the domestic and romantic lives of French and English Canadians before or just following the conquest. Her biographer has suggested that her major novels can be read as attempts to resolve historical conflicts between the "two nations" by explaining the feelings and intentions of each to the other.

However, the best-known and influential fictional historical character in nineteenth-century Canada was American poet Henry Wadsworth Longfellow's Evangeline, the main character in his 1847 poem, "Evangeline: A Tale of Acadie." Told in two parts, "Evangeline" tells the story of a young couple, Evangeline and her fiancé Gabriel, who in the first part of the poem grow up in the idyllic setting of Grand-Pré. Their happiness is shattered in the poem's second part with the British expulsion of the Acadians (1755–63). Both are sent on separate ships to the thirteen colonies and Evangeline spends the rest of her life searching for Gabriel. In the end they are reunited in Philadelphia where Evangeline, having become a Sister of Mercy, is nursing the sick. In the midst of a smallpox epidemic, she finds Gabriel on his deathbed, where he dies in her arms. Although Longfellow wrote his poem as a testimony to female fidelity and devotion, over the course of the nineteenth century it took on a number of other meanings for different audiences.

In 1865, Quebec's Pamphile LeMay translated "Evangeline" into French, and in 1887, during a period of Acadian cultural renewal, Acadian journalist Valentin Landry named his newspaper *L'Evangeline*, a name which it carried until its demise in 1982. As well as becoming an important symbol of Acadian survival and strength, by the late nineteenth century, the figure of Evangeline also turned up in tourist guidebooks, the Dominion Atlantic Railway Company's promotional literature, and on the chocolate boxes of New Brunswick confectioners Ganong Brothers.

Written texts, whether prose or poetry, were not the only ways in which British North Americans sought to define their relationship to the past and, in turn, their own identities. By the end of the nineteenth century, both English and French Canada were crafting historical narratives in multiple locations and genres: monuments, historical pageants, historical societies, and school textbooks and readers. However, before the efflorescence of these activities, French Canada had developed another artistic genre of creating its past – the historical painting. This was not, of course, a new form of art or unique to Lower Canada; Benjamin West's 1771 *The Death of General Wolfe*, for example, had been very popular when exhibited at London's Royal Academy. Historical paintings of significant moments in New France's history also existed alongside other genres, such as landscape art, portraits, cityscapes of Montreal's markets and streets, and religious paintings, all of which represented a growing market of both artists and audiences from the 1820s to the 1850s. Artists such as James Duncan (1806–1881), Théophile Hamel (1817–1870), Joseph Légaré (1795–1855), and Antoine Plamondon (1804–1895) took as their subjects events such as the deaths of Jesuit priests Jean de Brébeuf and Gabriel Lalement, the "massacre" of the Hurons by the Iroquois, Jacques Cartier's meeting with the Stadaconans (Samuel C. Hawksett, 1859), or the battle of Sainte-Foy. Duncan was born in Ireland and came to Lower

Canada in 1830, where he settled in Montreal and made a living as a drawing-master and artist. Hamel, Légaré, and Plamondon were all born in Quebec and created much of their work in Quebec City; Légaré was also active in the Quebec Literary and Historical Society. As well as representing a growing interest in the province's history among its urban middle class, these paintings also provided a basis for the late-nineteenth-century historical paintings that would become very popular in Quebec. Such art created a pantheon of heroism, both secular – the Comte de Frontenac, Madeleine de Verchères, Samuel de Champlain, Jacques Cartier, Dollard des Ormeaux, Generals Montcalm and Wolfe – and sacred – Marie de l'Incarnation, Marguerite d'Youville, Jeanne Mance, Bishop Laval, Catherine Tekakwitha, and, of course, the Jesuit martyrs. The elevation of these figures was also conducted in written texts and in monuments.

Other cultural forms and public demonstrations of identity were becoming increasingly common in British North America. Residents of Halifax, Saint John, Quebec City, Montreal, Ottawa, and Toronto might be entertained and educated by the sight of a number of their fellow citizens parading through the city's streets. Those who belonged to the societies or organizations which took to the streets to mark historic or festive events usually did so as a means of displaying particular religious, ethnic, or cultural affiliation, whether as members of the Orange Lodge, or the St. Andrew's (Scotland), St. George's (England), and St. Patrick's (Ireland) Societies. The latter three groups used public displays of marching and parading as a way of demonstrating their ties to their respective homelands, doing so on public holidays such as Queen Victoria's birthday in May. For their part, the Orange Lodge had made it part of their "tradition," particularly in Toronto but in cities in the Maritimes as well, to hold marches to observe significant events, such as the 1688 siege of Londonderry and the defeat of the Catholic King of England, James II, by the

Protestant King William III-William of Orange at the Battle of the Boyne, 12 July 1688. Some celebrations underwent a shift in their meaning and purpose over the course of the nineteenth century. For example, from the 1830s to the 1850s in Lower Canada, Saint-Jean-Baptiste Day (24 June) developed different meanings. Before the Rebellion, *Patriotes* marked the day with banquets and political debates. However, during the 1840s, the feast day took on a more distinctly religious tone, as it was observed with processions to and from mass; by 1885, religious and nationalist enthusiasms dominated the celebrations. In Toronto, St. Patrick's Day festivities also changed in their tone. Originally celebrated by Irish Protestants in eighteenth-century Ireland, by the 1840s, St. Patrick's Day became a predominantly religious and Catholic celebration. The focal point of the day was attendance at mass and the celebrations were organized by the church. By the late 1850s, though, the city's Irish Catholic laity had taken charge of the St. Patrick's Day events, which centred on a large, well-attended parade in which symbols of Irish nationalism, such as shamrocks and harps, predominated. Along with parades organized around these kinds of identities, British North Americans also participated in public displays for specific causes, such as temperance or the abolition of slavery in the United States, and to welcome prominent persons, such as the Prince of Wales during his North American tour of 1860.

As well as parades with their public display of symbols and images that linked participants and spectators to particular histories, a small, yet growing, number of British North Americans busied themselves with the establishment of museums. These were not yet the large, primarily state-supported institutions found in Britain or European countries, such as the British Museum. Until the establishment of the Royal Ontario Museum in Toronto in 1914, most museums in the Canadas and the Maritimes were smaller collections, often organized at the local level by particular individuals or organizations, such as Mechanics' Institutes, religious orders or denominations, colleges and universities, scientific societies, and private collectors. Moreover, while the 1830s saw the spread of such collections, in French Canada they had even longer roots, as seminaries in New France had collected objects since the mid-seventeenth century, with the founding of the Séminaire de Québec. The Institut Canadien, founded in Montreal in 1844 as a debating society and lending library that focused on social and political concerns, opened a museum in 1854, while the Mechanics' Institute in Halifax merged with the province's Provincial Museum in 1861. Although their founders came from a range of backgrounds, these groups shared a widespread, transatlantic interest in collecting objects as a means of understanding the past and conducting research through the study of artefacts. In Upper Canada, the links between collecting and public education were exemplified by the province's superintendent of education, Egerton Ryerson, who in 1857 set up an Educational Museum in the Toronto Normal School (the province's teacher-training institution). Influenced by his extensive travels in Britain and Europe in the 1840s and 1850s, where he had been exposed to ideas about the use of objects in teaching, Ryerson assembled copies of well-known paintings and sculptures, as well as armour and weapons, agricultural implements, and death masks.

He also provided the museum with scientific models, photographs, and natural history specimens, an interest that he shared with a number of his contemporaries. Ryerson's fascination with natural history was widely shared across nineteenth-century Canada, as well as in the United States and Britain. The New Brunswick Natural History Society, formed in Saint John in 1862, began displaying its collection of minerals, fossils, marine invertebrates, insects, plants, and stuffed birds two years later. The Society's founders were exclusively male professionals with an interest in areas such as geology or botany, who wished to present the province's natural history to both its residents and visitors. Like other natural history museums in Canada, such as Montreal's Redpath Museum, the Saint John Museum presented its objects in glass cases or on shelves; it did not create the kinds of dioramic displays favoured by institutions such as New York's American Museum of Natural History, which placed objects in a simulated environment. Instead, the New Brunswick Society's members thought that an understanding of natural history was best developed through careful, close, and direct observation of the objects themselves, whether within the confines of the building's displays or in the forests and fields of the province. The Society also worked with schools to educate children in natural history and to teach them about science through techniques such as drawing and collecting. It also sought to make the study of natural history of practical use to agriculture and business, as it promoted scientific agricultural education and argued for a need to recognize natural resources that would assist the provincial economy (the Society's artefacts became the base of the New Brunswick Museum's collection, founded in 1929). In Quebec and Ontario, organizations such as Montreal's Natural History Society (1827), the Geological Survey of Canada (1842), and Toronto's Canadian Institute (1851) played a central role in helping establish areas such as natural history, archaeology, and ethnography.

Other collectors focused on history, albeit from particular perspectives, and assembled objects that reflected their sense of the past. David Ross McCord (1844–1930), for example, the Montreal-based lawyer best known for his role as a collector, started his collection in his home, Temple Grove. McCord focused on military artefacts, both of British soldiers (the largest collection in the world of material relating to General Wolfe) and First Nations leaders (Joseph Brant's skull, Tecumseh's war bonnet), thus creating a history of masculine martial prowess, an experience far removed from his own. McCord's was a comprehensive collection since, along with material on Aboriginal people,

British imperialism, and the fur trade, he also amassed thousands of books and pamphlets (in 1921, his collection would become the McCord Museum). In the Ontario village of Niagara-on-the-Lake, located at the mouth of the Niagara River, local historian and retired teacher Janet Carnochan was a central figure in assembling a collection of 5,000 artefacts that dealt with the area's Loyalists, the War of 1812, the "pioneer past," and the town's history (it also included objects from across Canada, South Africa, India, and Britain). Starting in 1901, Carnochan presided over the collection and played a leading part in efforts that led to the construction of Memorial Hall to house it. With the Hall's opening in 1907, the Niagara Historical Society's collection became the first in Ontario to be housed in its own museum.

Museums and galleries also shared the mid-nineteenth century's concern with displaying the fruits of industrial and commercial capitalism, one that spread across Britain, western Europe, and through much of North America. The department store, for example, became a place in which many types of goods, displayed in ways to tempt consumers, could be bought under one roof; establishments such as Paris's *Bon Marché* or London's Harrod's and Whiteley's ("The Universal Provider") became well-known tourist attractions. Even more closely related to museums were the large exhibitions that flourished in late-nineteenth- and early twentieth-century cities. Starting with London's Crystal Palace in 1851, displays of goods and, at times, people in national and international exhibitions told narratives of national progress and prosperity achieved in industry, commerce, and agriculture.

British North Americans and Canadians participated in exhibitions "at home" and abroad. At the Philadelphia Centennial Exhibition of 1876, for example, Ontario's Education Department sent models of schools, scientific apparatuses, and teaching aids such as globes and maps. It took home a number of medals and sparked the Japanese government's interest; the latter purchased almost all the educational equipment. At the provincial level, in late June 1899, the Ontario Historical Society sponsored a three-day historical exhibition, held at Victoria University at the University of Toronto. Spread over seven different rooms, the "Historical," as the press dubbed it, displayed portraits, photographs, furniture, household items, weapons and military uniforms (some of them from imperial conflicts in India, Egypt, Afghanistan, and Burma), clothing, maps, books, pamphlets, and autographs. While its organizers had gathered collections from Montreal, Winnipeg, and Newfoundland, many of the items displayed related to the Upper Canadian political and social elite; they also were meant to convey narratives of the province's commercial and industrial development. Although much of the exhibition focused on objects used primarily by men, a separate room was set aside for "the Ladies," which featured decorative work and handicrafts (dresses, shawls, slippers, bedspreads, and tablecloths) and the tools used to make them (a tatting shuttle, pincushions, and workboxes). While this display suggests conventional, middle-class notions of femininity, it belied the central role that women played in organizing the Historical Exhibition, particularly that of the Women's Canadian Historical Society of Toronto (the latter was so active that some members of the Ontario History Society grumbled to each other that the women have taken over and had pushed aside the men). As well as the displays, the many visitors to the exhibit could enjoy lectures, concerts and a children's chorus, cadet corps displays, and garden parties. In Victoria's classrooms and grounds, education and entertainment came together.

Visitors could also be entertained by the delegation of Six Nations chiefs, who came to the opening day. While the great majority of exhibitions focused on the present and future, significant narratives of Canada's past, both in the Historical Exhibition and in other venues, were told through the artefacts of Aboriginal people. At times, these narratives focused on the triumph of the Canadian state's assimilationist policies in banishing "primitive savagery" and replacing it with "civilization." In Western Canada, for example, the Dominion government sponsored agricultural exhibitions on reserves that displayed the fruits of Aboriginal agriculture or gave prizes at white exhibitions for First Nations' produce. Some First Nations people ran their own exhibitions; the Six Nations at the Grand River reserve near Brantford, Ontario, formed an agricultural society in 1868 and held competitions restricted to Indigenous entrants. As well, during the 1850s, Aboriginal artefacts formed an important component of the goods sent by government officials to international exhibitions in London and Paris. Although such artefacts became less popular with government officials in the following decade, as they believed that these items undermined the state's efforts to display Indigenous people as assimilated, during the 1870s, such artefacts experienced a resurgence of interest, as anthropologists and private collectors sent in ethnographic materials for display. Indigenous people themselves sometimes appeared in exhibitions; in 1893 at the Chicago World Fair, groups of Inuit and Kwakwa'wakw people stayed in their own encampments.

Historians have debated Indigenous people's participation in these types of displays, asking if they were coerced into participating, if they exercised any degree of control over their representations, and if their participation had results that the organizers did not foresee, such as preserving cultural rituals that might otherwise have been lost or suppressed by missionaries and the state (similar questions have been asked about their participation in photography and performances such as Wild West shows). We have far fewer examples, though, of First Nations people in Canada who organized their own museum displays and acted as "collectors." One striking exception, though, was Dr. Oronhyatekha (Peter Martin) (1841–1908), a Mohawk from Six Nations who studied medicine at Oxford and the University of Toronto, who worked as a merchant and farmer, and from 1881 to 1907 was a leading figure in the International Order of Foresters, an insurance organization. Equally importantly, Oronhyatekha amassed a collection of 800 objects that spanned natural history, material pertaining to the International Order of Foresters, his travels to Fiji, New Guinea, Australia, Japan, and Burma, and Indigenous history of the Great Lakes and Eastern Woodlands, Plains, and Arctic. By acquiring existing collections and enlisting the help of other collectors, Oronhyatekha expressed his own diverse range of interests, experiences, and beliefs. In particular, by including Indigenous objects that dealt with a period in which they had been leaders of sovereign nations (items that belonged to Tecumseh or clothing that chiefs had worn when visiting British royalty), Oronhyatekha demonstrated his conviction that the Iroquois were the equals of Europeans. Oronhyatekha's collection is a fascinating example of Indigenous people's response to European culture in the nineteenth century. Far from allowing themselves to be simply historical artefacts, they engaged with non-Indigenous culture but manipulated it for their own ends and interests. Such a response can also be found during the "heyday" of commemorative activities in late-nineteenth- and early-twentieth-century Canada.

Crafting "a past" in British North America and nineteenth-century Canada relied, then, on a variety of approaches to the creation of historical knowledge. Multiple influences shaped this plurality of genres and methodologies. Material conditions – the growth of the colonial middle class, the spread of formal education, networks of voluntary societies, and faster transportation and communication systems – made it possible for colonists to come together to discuss and promote their respective histories. Furthermore, influences from south of the border, such as Parkman's work or Longfellow's poetry, made their way into British North America's conceptions of the colonial past. These developments simultaneously helped shape colonial sensibilities, a process in which the importance of making histories, whether of one's religion, ethnicity, and region, began to play an increasingly significant role. Widespread imperial and international processes were important; ideas about the need to write one's history as a way of forging identity were brought either by recent immigrants to the colonies or disseminated through print culture in the transatlantic world of Britain, Europe, and the United States. To be sure, such ideas were not new. First Nations and African-Canadians, for example, had long understood the necessity of transmitting communal and personal memories, particularly when faced by the political, economic, and cultural upheavals brought about by encounters with Europeans. As well as continuing to rely on older oral traditions of narrating their pasts, they too made use of print culture, sometimes interweaving the former into the fabric of written texts. Locating oneself in place and time became an increasingly crucial means of self-definition in British North America; it would become even more so as the former colonies began to see themselves as the Dominion of Canada.

3

The Heyday of Public Commemorations in Canada, 1870s–1920s

While written texts were crucially important in creating a shared sense of the past and collective memory during the nineteenth century, they were far from being the only genre of public history. The last third of the nineteenth century in Canada witnessed the rise of a number of commemorative activities that flourished well into the 1920s; it is not an exaggeration to describe this period as consisting of the "heyday of public commemorations." Across Quebec, Ontario, and the Maritimes, Canadians erected monuments, staged historical pageants, and formed historical societies in efforts to remember and mark specific events and individuals; this interest in celebrating the past also spread to Newfoundland, the Prairies, and British Columbia.

To some extent, Canadians were influenced by developments in other countries, as Britain, the United States, and much of western Europe witnessed a similar wave of attempts to remember the past in very public and visual ways. In the United States, for example, Civil War veterans and their supporters came together from the 1880s on to remember the conflict. Public pageants in Britain or America, whether devoted to town histories or to events deemed to be nationally significant, were staged by groups that ranged from local historical societies to national (sometimes transnational) movements, such as the women's suffrage campaign of the early twentieth century. Scholars have debated the reasons for this flurry of commemorative work and have suggested a number of motivations for the commemorators. In some cases, selective memories of an event clearly helped produce a historical narrative that was used to bind together former enemies in the name of national unity and racial identity. For example, in the case of the U.S. Civil War, both Confederate and Union veterans and their supporters put up almost identical monuments to white soldiers and insisted that the war had been about "states' rights." Their commemorations thus attempted to erase the place of slavery in American history and denied African-Americans' struggle for emancipation, thereby creating an American history marked by unity, not deep divisions. At other times, historical narratives were used to provide legitimation and inspiration, as when suffragists staged pageants that featured heroic and important female figures from history, such as Elizabeth I, the anti-Roman Queen Boadicea, or Joan of Arc.

For some white, upper-middle-class urban elites in the United States, the late nineteenth century was a time of great anxiety about urbanization, immigration, and industrialization. The past appeared to provide them with a welcome refuge from widespread social, cultural, and political changes and challenges, a phenomenon that has been called "antimodernism." For these people, either society had experienced a steady but inexorable decline in the modern era, or a direct and clear rupture with the past had occurred. Whatever the case, though, they contrasted the late nineteenth century with either a colonial or, for some, medieval past in which social relationships were much simpler and straightforward, often marked by clear lines of hierarchy so far as gender, race, and class relations were concerned. On the other hand, there were those commemorators who believed that the history of their country, province, region, or locality had been full of progressive achievements that continued into the present and should be celebrated.

As well as cultural and intellectual factors, changing social and economic conditions led to greater participation in public history. For one, the development of railroads and steamships brought greater numbers of people together, both as participants in and as witnesses to large-scale acts of commemoration. Improved transportation networks also made it easier to transport materials for statues and monuments and the designs to execute them. A growing middle class, from whose ranks most of the commemorators came, also had the time to pursue historical knowledge, often on a purely voluntary basis; they also had the connections and ability to lobby their counterparts and, at times, various levels of government for funding and other forms of support. Not surprisingly, the political and social context of monument building, then, meant that those chosen for commemoration tended to reflect the desires and aspirations of particular groups in Canadian society. While commemorators in Canada were influenced by international developments – historical societies, for example, often exchanged papers and records with similar groups in the United States – the national context also shaped their work. In Canada, the wave of commemorative activities of the late nineteenth and early twentieth century also occurred during a period historians have characterized as being that of "nation building": for example, the transcontinental railroad was completed and increased numbers of European immigrants arrived in Western Canada; the three Prairie provinces joined Confederation; the Dominion government expanded its departments and, in particular, intensified its control over Aboriginal communities; and leading Canadian intellectuals in both French and English Canada debated and discussed national identity and the country's relationships to both Britain and the United States. Building monuments, forming historical societies, and staging pageants were also part of this context.

Monuments, however, began to appear in the British North American colonies long before there was a "Canada."

The monument to Britain's Admiral Nelson, for example, that stands in Montreal's Place Jacques-Cartier was erected in 1809, four years after the Battle of Trafalgar, where he was mortally wounded. One of the first such edifices to the Admiral's memory (others were erected in Glasgow and Edinburgh in 1806 and 1815), it was financed by publicly raised money, a drive organized by a committee that included prominent, wealthy English-speaking members of the city's political and commercial elite. Not only was the monument placed in an important civic centre, it also looked down on Montreal's pillory, which municipal authorities moved to the monument's base, thus linking recent past glory to public punishment. In 1828, residents of Quebec City saw the erection of an obelisk to the opposing generals of the Battle of the Plains of Abraham, James Wolfe and Louis-Joseph de Montcalm. Initiated by Governor General Lord Dalhousie, the monument was intended to inspire unity between French and English as much as it was meant to honour the two men. Three decades later, at the suggestion of French-Canadian nationalist Georges-Barthélemi Faribault, Montcalm would receive his own monument in Quebec City, erected on the 100th anniversary of the battle.

In Upper Canada, one of the earliest and most prominent monuments in British North America was put up to honour British military leader Isaac Brock, who died at the Battle of Queenston Heights in October 1812. The history of Brock's monument clearly illustrates the political dimensions of commemoration. Along with his aide John Macdonell, Brock was first buried in Queenston; Upper Canadians made attempts to commemorate him with a monument at Queenston Heights once the War of 1812 ended. The colony's legislative assembly voted to spend £1,000 for its construction in 1815 and, in 1820, set aside an additional £6,000 for its completion. Thousands attended the unveiling in 1824 of a column that reached 135 feet (41 metres) and provided those who made the climb with an observation platform that looked over the Niagara River.

The monument also became a gravesite, as Brock and Macdonell were buried in its base. In 1840, though, reformer Alexander Lett, who had supported rebel leader William Lyon Mackenzie in 1837, attempted to blow up the monument; while Lett was unsuccessful, he managed to destroy its stairway and opened a crack in its side. Upper Canadians representing a range of political perspectives reacted swiftly: a mass meeting organized in 1840 by Lieutenant-Governor George Arthur brought together conservatives (Attorney-General John Beverley Robinson), moderate reformers (politician and businessman William Hamilton Merritt), militia officers, and War of 1812 veterans. Those who attended passed a resolution calling for a new monument, with funds to be supplied by a public subscription, not the provincial government. The subsequent campaign netted $50,000 and included donations from Aboriginal people – the Chippewa along the St. Clair River and in the Saugeen area, for example – along with expressions of outrage at Lett's actions. Not only did these communities remember their military contributions to the War of 1812, they also saw Mackenzie as being too fond of the United States government, with its policies of Indian removal and cruel treatment of Aboriginal people during the Revolution and in its aftermath. The new monument's completion, though, was a fairly lengthy process. It took two years before the design competition was announced and there were a number of delays afterwards. The new monument was not completed until 1853; however, it proved to be unlike any other statue in British North America and, quite possibly, in North America. Designed by Toronto architect John G. Howard, who worked with prominent Canadian builder William Thomas, Brock's monument was now a 184-foot (56-metre) Corinthian column topped by a sixteen-foot statue, its large, imposing base composed of rough-hewn stones that contrasted with the column's smooth lines. The monument in both of its incarnations was not only an important commemorative marker; it also became a major tourist attraction.

The landscapes of Ontario and Quebec in particular were dotted with monuments during the late nineteenth and early twentieth century. From the 1880s to the 1920s, Canadians, French and English, worked diligently to construct monuments that honoured explorers, religious figures, military leaders, and, in some cases, politicians. Although governments at the Dominion, provincial, and local levels were involved in these efforts, quite often the initiative for these statues came from middle-class and secular voluntary organizations, sometimes with the support of religious denominations. Almost all the figures chosen for public commemoration were male; with a few important exceptions, almost all were of European descent. In Quebec, explorers and religious leaders were sometimes coupled as a way of commemorating New France's French and Catholic origins. In 1889, residents of Quebec City saw a statue erected to honour both Jacques Cartier and the seventeenth-century Jesuit missionaries, such as Jean de Brébeuf, killed by the Iroquois at Sainte-Marie-among-the-Hurons. Nine years later, in 1898, the statues of Cartier and the Jesuits were joined by a monument to Samuel de Champlain. In 1908, the city also hosted a three-day celebration of Bishop Laval, first bishop of Quebec, on the bicentenary of his death, that involved large public processions of priests, nuns, bishops, civil leaders, and professors; a large open-air mass, and the unveiling of a monument. After the religious ceremonies had come to a close, the Société St-Jean-Baptiste-de-Québec (SSJBQ) sponsored a display of athletic games intended, along with the Laval commemorations, to highlight and celebrate French Canadians' strong religious beliefs and their "racial" prowess. This was not the first time the Bishop was commemorated, though. In 1878, following the discovery of his long-lost coffin, the Catholic Church honoured Laval with a very formal and highly orchestrated ceremony of reburial, one that was held over a number of days and that involved multiple public processions with both religious and secular participants.

Through these multiple commemorative events, Laval went from being one of the lesser-known figures in New France's history to a significant historical actor. As well as tributes to New France's "founding fathers," British monarchy was also honoured, as statues of, first, Queen Victoria (an important exception to the masculinity of Canadian monuments) and then of her successor, King Edward VII, were built in a number of Canadian cities. Another "father," in this case of Confederation, was memorialized in 1895 with the unveiling of Sir John A. Macdonald's statue in Montreal's Dominion Square only four years after the former prime minister's death. Such monuments were, of course, a way of demarcating and claiming public space; they expressed their founders' concepts of "Canada" and reminded spectators of a particular vision of the country's past. They also helped to create a site of remembrance in a very public way, both in initial unveiling ceremonies and subsequently during significant anniversaries, when processions might be held to them, speeches made honouring the subject of the monument, and wreaths laid. In the case of many of Quebec's monuments, they brought together the realms of the sacred and the secular. A number of Catholic nationalists, for example, saw Laval as an important religious leader and the creator of modern Quebec.

However, although monuments were meant to serve as symbols of unity, their construction also might bring out rivalries and political animosities, stirring up strong emotions in the process. The Catholic Church, for example, counted on receiving much more financial support from the laity for Laval's monument than it received. In 1908, when the SSJBQ wanted to commemorate Champlain, it found that its work was taken over by Earl Grey, the governor general, and the Catholic Church. As well, certain figures might become less popular in the public imagination, a fate suffered by Champlain and Laval who eventually saw their stars eclipsed by the "hero" of the Long-Sault, Adam Dollard des Ormeaux. Dollard des Ormeaux, sent in 1660 by Montreal's governor on a mission up the Ottawa River with French companions and an Indigenous contingent, ran into an Iroquois hunting band; the ensuing conflict resulted in Dollard des Ormeaux's and his companions' deaths. Although historians now believe that Dollard des Ormeaux was sent either to rob the Iroquois of their furs or to accompany French traders back to Montreal, in the twentieth century, Quebec historian Lionel Groulx claimed that Dollard des Ormeaux and his companions were resisting an Iroquois invasion; therefore, the incident should be seen as a pivotal episode in the defence of French Canada.

Moreover, just as other forms of public history involved certain types of choices about which parts of the past were acceptable – and which were to be downplayed or forgotten – so too did the construction of monuments. The memorialization of the *Patriotes*, for example, demonstrates how certain historical actors could take on different meanings, depending upon the context of their memorialization and those who undertook to remember them. In 1858, a statue was raised in Montreal to honour *Patriote* leader Ludger Duvernay; its unveiling drew an audience of over 10,000 spectators. However, they were not told of his role in the Rebellion, which led him to flee to the United States. Rather, Duvernay was remembered as playing a pivotal role in founding the Saint-Jean-Baptiste Association. This case of selective memory is perhaps not surprising, as the statue was built by the Association's members, men whose conservative politics led them to shun the liberalism and secularism of the Rebellion and who did not want their founder to be linked to it. Other statues to the *Patriotes* demonstrate the shifting meanings of the Rebellion within the province's public memory. In 1895, the Institut Canadien put up a statue of Jean-Olivier Chénier, an important *Patriote* leader. The statue is simple: it features Chénier holding a musket and urging his men on; the inscription reads "Chenier, 1837, 1895." Unlike the Duvernay monument's unveiling ceremony, only a few hundred attended that of the Chénier statue; by 1895, those who wished to remember him and his compatriots as secular republicans had become a minority in the province. By 1926, though, when an obelisk to the *Patriotes* was erected on the site of the prison in which they had been jailed, things had changed. Both the Catholic Church and the Saint-Jean-Baptiste society supported the monument and had the site renamed the *Place des Patriotes*. In the ceremony and on the obelisk, which featured allegorical representations of liberty, Chénier and his compatriots were remembered as martyrs in the cause of French-Canadian nationalism. No longer threats to church and state, they were now heroes, claimed as such in the aftermath of Quebec's political and social leaders' struggles against conscription, a campaign which had brought together the clergy and liberal politicians.

Furthermore, unlike the situation in, for example, France, where the same figure – often a prominent politician – might be memorialized in multiple statues, in Quebec a greater variety and range of statues were put up. Until the early 1920s, only a few figures were repeated in the province's list of monuments, such as the politician George-Étienne Cartier, Queen Victoria, and Prime Minister Wilfrid Laurier. Quebec displayed a much greater range of figures with local and provincial meanings. Very few statues were erected to politicians from outside the province, with the exceptions of Upper Canadian politician Robert Baldwin and Prime Minister John A. Macdonald. Most of the statues were of male figures; few of the better-known women from the province's history were honoured in statuary. Between them, Joan of Arc and Queen Victoria were memorialized more frequently than, for example, Catherine Tekakwitha, Jeanne Mance, and Madeleine de Verchères (there also was a cairn put up to the memory of Lady Head, wife of the 1830s lieutenant-governor, Sir Francis Bond Head). Overall, though, memorials were far more likely to use female imagery in allegorical form, a pattern that was not, by any means, unique to Quebec.

Ontario's "monument craze" occurred at the same time as that of Quebec's but differed somewhat in its subjects. Perhaps the most striking distinction between the two provinces was the greater emphasis placed on secular leaders by Ontario's monument builders. Statues were put up for a few religious figures, such as the Methodists' Egerton Ryerson and Eastern Ontario Loyalist Barbara Heck – the latter memorialized as the "mother of Methodism" for her role in bringing the faith to Upper Canada. However, they also were remembered for their roles in other capacities. Ryerson was celebrated as the founder of Ontario public education; although Heck's religious identity was certainly central to her memorialization, she also was seen as a Loyalist. Moreover, public versions of history in Ontario became dominated by three historical narratives: the Loyalist migration and their role in "founding" the province, the War of 1812, and the pioneer past. From the 1880s until the outbreak of the First World War, the Loyalists and the War of 1812 were particularly central to Ontario's memorial landscape.

While these late-nineteenth-century monuments were clearly meant to help create national histories, paying close attention to the history of their building shows us that the "nation" and the "state" were not always the same entity; often the state, or government, was a reluctant partner when it came to committing funds. In Ontario, although monuments were constructed with the moral support of the provincial government, the latter rarely took the initiative in spearheading drives for the memorialization of particular individuals or events. It was far more common for the government to act in response to pressure from voluntary groups, such as the historical societies which, beginning in the 1880s, were founded across southern Ontario, along with the United Empire Loyalist Association, formed in 1896. (In this, Ontario lagged behind New Brunswick, which had held its own Loyalist celebrations in 1883, with re-enactments in Saint John of their arrival and the erection of various monuments across the city to Loyalist history.) The Association became the largest patriotic and hereditary group in Ontario, its goals both to celebrate the Loyalists and to ensure that their legacy lived on in the province. The Association was run by Toronto-based middle-class professionals, almost all of whom were Anglicans, and whose politics were conservative in their support of British imperialism, suspicious of immigrants and Americans, and zealous in their desire to have their particular interpretation of Canadian history taught in the province's schools. Many members were professional men and white-collar workers, although 51 per cent of the group were middle-class women, such as feminist and writer Mary Edgar, who wished to ensure that Loyalist women's contributions were recognized and honoured along with those of Loyalist men. Moreover, in 1898, the Association invited Six Nations chiefs Jacob Salem Johnson and Sampson Green to become honorary vice-presidents and admitted the entire communities of Six Nations and Tyendinaga as associate members. According to genealogist and lawyer E.M. Chadwick, these communities' support for the Crown needed to be recognized as having made a significant contribution to the Loyalist cause. For their part, the Six Nations saw the gesture as important, both for the history that it honoured but also for its contemporary political implications in their struggle against the limitations of the Indian Act. Running their own historical societies suggested that they were capable of running their own affairs more broadly; it also might provide them with important elite allies who could support them in their negotiations with the Dominion government.

While historic societies shared a common goal – preserving and celebrating the province's past – their motivations for doing so varied. While the United Empire Loyalist Association demonstrated elite antimodern anxieties about industrialization or urbanization, members of other historical organizations seem to have been less preoccupied with such fears, their work marked by a greater sense of confidence about Canada's direction. Moreover, although they can be described as middle class – historical societies do not appear to have included working-class men and women – that did not mean these groups should be seen as homogenous. While organizations such as the Kingston Historical Society, which included a number of Queen's University professors and well-off professional figures, tended to have a greater number of intellectual, political, and social elites, societies outside of larger urban centres tended to include a greater spectrum of less-prosperous or less well-connected businessmen, professionals, and politicians. Ontario's historical societies also included a number of influential women's organizations, such as the St. Catharines Women's Literary Club, the Women's Canadian Historical Societies of Toronto and Ottawa, and the Wentworth Women's Historical Society. Those single women who were active in these groups – Sarah Curzon, Janet Carnochan, Augusta Gilkison, and Harriett Priddis – often found it a struggle to come up with the funds for travel to provincial meetings or to make a living as writers of historical prose and drama.

Like historical commemoration in Quebec, Loyalist commemorations were not without their own conflicts and divisions. In 1884, for example, a date chosen to remember the arrival of the Loyalists in Upper Canada, celebrations of the Loyalist arrival at Adolphustown on the shores of eastern Lake Ontario were marked by divisions between Anglicans and Methodists. Each denomination attempted to claim a place for itself as the most important actor within the province's history. Certain figures claimed by Loyalist promoters might have different meanings for different groups. For example, the Mohawk leader Joseph Brant, for whom a statue was erected in the centre of the southern Ontario town of Brantford in 1886, was a complicated historical figure. Because Brant had allied himself with the Crown during the American Revolution, for non-Aboriginal Loyalists he could be a symbol of Aboriginal support for the Crown, Aboriginal submission to the British presence in

North America, and assimilation to British ways. However, for some members of the Six Nations Confederacy, particularly Christian Mohawks, Brant was a savvy and astute political leader of vision and diplomacy who had his own reasons for supporting the British and coming to Canada. Other members of the Confederacy, particularly those who practised the traditional Longhouse religion, were opposed to celebrating the memory of someone that they believed had betrayed them and created a rift within the Confederacy; not all the Iroquois had aligned themselves with the British and many remained within the new republic. (Such divisions over Brant's legacy can still be found among Iroquois communities today.) Whatever one's stance on Brant, another, equally notable feature of his commemoration was historians' general silence on the subject of his sister, Mary or Molly Brant. As the partner of the eighteenth-century British colonial official, Indian Superintendent Sir William Johnson, historians credit Mary Brant as having possessed diplomatic skills that were equal to her brother's, a key figure in maintaining the Confederacy's alliance with the British. While over the course of the twentieth century non-Aboriginals would begin to honour Mary Brant, she still does not receive the attention paid to Joseph.

The commemoration of the Loyalists was also marked by its participants' need to create a unifying history out of very disparate elements. The men and women who arrived in Canada in the 1770s and 1780s were not a unified group: they were a diverse mix of those of British and European descent and included Aboriginals, freed Blacks, and slaves. Moreover, historians know very little about many of the Loyalists' motives for coming to Canada, since few who arrived in Upper Canada left written records concerning their reasons for supporting the Crown. Not all those who arrived in British North America were an elite, as many upper-class Loyalists had gone to England. While a small group of officers arrived in Upper Canada, many of the Loyalists were farmers and artisans. Some may well have been committed to the preservation of British Empire; others, though, were motivated by economic reasons, such as patronage ties or commercial links to Britain. Still others were opportunistic and took pledges of allegiance to whichever side appeared to be winning, while another group probably would have preferred to have remained neutral but were harassed by both Patriots and Loyalists and took oaths of loyalty to escape further intimidation. However, this more complicated history was either unknown to their commemorators or ignored. Instead, the reports of the historical societies, the publications of the United Empire Loyalist Association, and monuments to the Loyalists created a Loyalist "tradition" that featured narratives and images of unswerving devotion to King and Empire, of physical and emotional sacrifice, and of a strong moral and Christian character.

Linked to the Loyalists was the militia of 1812. Narratives and images of the War of 1812 stressed the militia's steadfast devotion to Britain and Upper Canada, its centrality to the Americans' defeat, and the place of Brock as a Christ-like (and Wolfe- and Nelson-like) hero who gave his life for his adopted country. To be sure, this narrative had a history of its own: it was promoted by colonial authorities during the war itself and, in its immediate aftermath, by organizations such as the Loyal and Patriotic Society of Upper Canada, which arranged compensations for civilians who had suffered losses and damages to property. However, the notion of the militia as having played a central role in Canada's creation became an even more prominent aspect of Upper Canadian history by the 1890s and 1900s; it could be found in the historical societies' narratives of historical societies, in school texts and readers, and in monuments. Like that of the Loyalists, though, these narratives tended to ignore or gloss over the role of British troops and Indigenous allies who nevertheless played a pivotal role in the conflict. They also omitted Brock's and the British military's concerns about the militia's high rates of absenteeism and, often, indifference to the war. Such narratives also overlooked the fact that, in the aftermath of the war, the colony was far from united by the militia's glorious defence of it. Upper Canadian society was marked by conflict over who would receive compensation for wartime losses and contributions, not to mention ongoing political and religious tensions.

However, narratives and images of the militia served a number of purposes, both immediately after the War of 1812 and in the 1880s and 1890s. For one, participating in or being affected by the war, either as soldier or civilian, was open to a broader group of Upper Canadians than United Empire Loyalist membership. Those who had come from Britain, such as the Anglican rector of York John Strachan, could claim that their wartime sacrifices made them worthy to occupy prominent and powerful positions in Upper Canadian society. Later in the century, not only did the War of 1812 continue to provide a number of Ontario residents with a history of loyal service to, and defense of, the British Empire, it was also viewed by many writers as a founding moment of the Canadian nation, since both Upper and Lower Canada, English and French, came together in military struggle and triumphed in repulsing a common enemy. The two "founding races" thus were seen as having acted as a national community. Of course, this narrative glossed over the fact that the war had far less of an impact on the Maritimes, where narratives of the Loyalists, particularly in New Brunswick, were much more influential. It also overlooked the historical reality that nation building was not part of the war: Upper Canada was simply one of many colonial outposts that required defence as part of a much larger global conflict between Britain, the new American republic, and France.

Despite all of this, though, the war also rescued the Loyalists from the suggestion that, as defeated refugees, they might be seen as history's losers. The War of 1812 could thus be portrayed as a triumph for Upper Canadian manhood and, by extension, for their male descendants. Female historians, such as Curzon, Mary Agnes Fitzgibbon, Carnochan,

and St. Catharines resident Emma Currie, found in the figure of Laura Secord a heroine, one that they could claim for
her particular historic contribution (walking twenty miles
from Queenston to Beaverdams to warn the British troops
of an impending American attack) and for her more general qualities, such as devotion to her husband and children.
These commemorators perpetuated Secord's memory in
monuments at the Lundy's Lane cemetery in Niagara Falls
and at Queenston Heights, as well as in numerous articles,
books, and a play by Curzon.

   As well as monuments and other markers of historic sites,
Canadians in the late nineteenth and early twentieth century also participated in a very popular and public form of
commemoration, the historical pageant (which was sometimes held as part of a monument's unveiling and dedication). While pageants were ephemeral in that they did
not leave the same material traces on the landscape as did
monuments, a number of pageants nevertheless left written
and visual records such as programs, newspaper accounts,
records of organizing committees, and diaries left by participants and spectators. Depending on their reach and scope,
pageants might permit a greater range of people to participate than in the case of monuments, which often directly
involved a relatively smaller group of organizers (although
they might draw a sizable crowd for their unveiling). The
theatrical appeal of historical pageants helps account somewhat for their popularity, as they drew upon certain forms
of popular culture – theatre, parades, and festivals – and
had the potential to make history "come alive" for those
who acted in them and for their audiences.

   Just as monument-building was an international phenomenon, so too were pageants. Modern historical pageants date from the first decade of the twentieth century
and first took place in England. According to their English "founder," Louis Napoleon Parker, large-scale pageants should bring communities together in a number of
ways. Pageants should involve the entire community; their

participants would not only act in them but they also would make their own costumes and props, do the research for the scripts they wrote, compose the music, and be organizers, actors, and audience members (the community itself was the set). For its participants and audience, pageants would make the past live, acting as a kind of enchantment and escape from the humdrum nature of modern life. In the United States after the First World War, a number of pageants were held to mark the histories of small towns and cities and were intended to promote community cohesion and inculcate civic pride. In Britain, pageants were often held in conjunction with other major events – coronations, Jubilees, or opening of international exhibitions – and they often celebrated British nationalism and the British Empire.

The two largest and best-known Canadian pageants were the 1908 pageant held at Quebec City to mark the Tercentenary of Samuel de Champlain's founding of Quebec and those staged across Canada in 1927 to commemorate the Diamond Jubilee of Confederation. Both events were meant to celebrate the idea of the Canadian nation and to reinforce national pride and unity by presenting particular narratives of Canadian history. In many ways they were successful, as different groups of Canadians came together under the aegis of national celebrations and often received the pageants with great enthusiasm. However, when we look closely at both the organization of these events and what was displayed, we also can see that in some cases the participants had different motives than those of the organizers and national committees which oversaw them.

Furthermore, in the case of the Champlain Tercentenary celebrations, the organizers themselves had different, sometimes competing, motives for hosting them. Municipal politicians in Quebec City wanted to boost the local economy, which had been in decline for a number of decades. The governor general, Earl Grey, wanted a national and imperial festival that would bring together not only various levels of government, voluntary groups, and mass groups of individuals, but also unite English and French Canada together in a fusion of the "races." Prime Minister Wilfrid Laurier initially was cool to the entire project, as he believed that Grey's vision of "race fusion" would only incite conflict between French and English Canada. Laurier hoped instead to celebrate the 1909 opening of the Quebec Bridge, which would span the St. Lawrence River, a hope that was dashed in 1907 when the bridge collapsed. The prime minister was then persuaded to throw his support behind the Tercentenary.

The Champlain Tercentenary was a lavish, three-day program that involved multiple events: a gathering of naval warships on the St. Lawrence River, processions through the city's streets, fireworks, a massed military tattoo, a regatta, concerts, an open-air mass, state dinners, balls, and garden parties (it was also marked by the presence of the Prince of Wales). At the centre, though, was the historical pageant, which depicted certain events from the history of seventeenth-century New France and, to a lesser extent, Lower Canada. While the pageant also included the Battle of the Plains of Abraham, the actors did not fight. Instead, Wolfe and Montcalm acknowledged each other, and their armies joined and marched across the field while the band played "O Canada" and "God Save the King."

All of these events were orchestrated by Frank Lascelles, a professional director and pageant organizer brought in from England, supported by an organizing committee composed of businessmen, politicians, and university professors. Almost 5,000 people participated in the pageant; their ranks included business and professional elites, local women's groups, and the Catholic Church. Canadian Pacific Railroad agents recruited groups of Iroquois and Anishinabe people from communities near Montreal and Sault Ste. Marie, whose performances in the pageants' battles, as well as their family camps on the Plains of Abraham, were a central attraction. A number of Indigenous people had crafted professional careers as performers in Wild West Shows, an expertise they put to good use in the Tercentenary.

What types of narratives about Quebec and Canada's history did the pageant present? Much of it was selective and very romantic. It portrayed the Catholic Church as a central, ultramontane force, one in which the pope's authority dominated that of the secular power, a point underscored through the organizers' choice of religious music, elaborate costumes, and canopies. History, in the Champlain Tercentenary, became a morality tale, its central themes qualities such as heroism, grandeur, nobility, community harmony, Christian sacrifice, loyalty, and providential destiny. There was no sense of the texture of daily life for habitant men, women, and children, let alone Aboriginal people. Furthermore, any tensions between the English and the French were downplayed.

The 1908 pageant was not the first large-scale public celebration of Champlain's arrival in North America, though. Four years earlier in New Brunswick, under the aegis of the province's historical society, local politicians, writers, labour leaders, businessmen, the militia, and other members of voluntary societies banded together to organize events in Saint John commemorating Champlain's landing. They were motivated by a desire to link New Brunswick's history to that of Canadian history, as opposed to seeing it solely within the framework of regional or provincial narratives. Like Quebec's pageant, the 1904 commemoration mixed the contemporary – band concerts, sports, Boy's Brigade displays, fireworks, and illuminations – with a dramatized meeting between the Mi'kmaq and French. This piece of open-air theatre was an attempt to educate spectators about the friendly and beneficent relations that had marked Aboriginal-newcomer encounters, although the historical record suggests far more tension and conflict. As the Mi'kmaq were played by non-Aboriginal members of a local rowing club, though, in all likelihood the message

was lost on the province's Indigenous residents. The festivities also included a procession of Boer War veterans, the
dedication of a plaque to Champlain, and a 200-page special issue of the province's scholarly history journal, *Acadiensis*. The Saint John Tercentenary also featured religious
dimensions, as the province's Irish-Catholics held their own
celebrations that stressed the spiritual domain as a way of
remembering Champlain. Like their counterparts in Quebec, the clergy advised their flocks to think of Champlain
as bringing Christianity to "heathen savages" and paving
the way for the Catholic Church's establishment. However,
in New Brunswick it was not the province's Acadians that
made this link but, rather, its Irish-Catholic community.
Members of male Irish-Catholic organizations (the Ancient
Order of Hibernians, the Father Matthew Society, Saint
Malachy's Total Abstinence society, for example) paraded
through the streets to a mass held in the city's cathedral.
Six years after these events, Saint John became home to
its own Champlain monument, the impetus for it having
been generated by the 1904 celebrations. The province's
Historical Society had lobbied for such a statue from the
start of the decade and saw its wishes fulfilled when sculptor
Hamilton McCarthy's design was put in place in the city's
Queen Square, which overlooked the harbour. McCarthy
was no stranger to monuments and, in particular, statues
of Champlain, as he had designed South African war statues in Halifax and Charlottetown, the Annapolis Royal de
Monts memorial, and statues of Champlain for Ottawa and
Quebec.

While figures such as Champlain, Cartier, Laval, and
Brock achieved varying degrees of recognition in the new
Dominion, in Newfoundland (which at that point was not
part of Canada) during the 1890s, the commemoration of
the explorer John Cabot (Giovanni Caboto), who landed
in North America in 1497, generated both excitement and,
for some, controversy. Much of the impetus for celebrating Cabot was sparked by the 1892 public ceremonies in

the United States that marked the 400th anniversary of Christopher Columbus's arrival in the Americas, ceremonies that included the Chicago World's Fair, a national school holiday, and a five-day celebration in New York City. Cabot's legacy was a contested one; depending on their own national and regional affinities, American, British, and Canadian scholars claimed that he had landed on either the Labrador coast, or Maine, or Nova Scotia. However, prominent Newfoundland historians Judge Daniel Prowse and Roman Catholic Bishop Howley claimed that Cabot's landfall had occurred in Newfoundland (Prowse consistently claimed Bonavista as the site, while over his lifetime Howley offered a number of possibilities). To be sure, they also differed in their interpretations of Cabot's landing. Prowse, whose 1895 *History of Newfoundland* was for many years the most comprehensive study of the colony, saw Cabot as an integral linchpin that tied Newfoundland to England and made it the latter's first colony. For his part, Howley, the child of Irish immigrants and the first bishop of Newfoundland to be born in the colony, celebrated Cabot and his landing as a symbol of Newfoundland nationalism, one that might heal the colony's sectarian divides (Howley also was a published historian, as his *Ecclesiastical History* appeared in 1888).

The 1897, celebrations of Cabot's landing in Bonavista were also complicated by their timing. They coincided with Queen Victoria's Diamond Jubilee, an event which some Newfoundlanders believed should take precedence over Cabot's commemoration. The Jubilee celebrations, held on 22 June, were organized primarily by elite women of St. John's; they included church services, fireworks, a naval review, gun salutes, and the laying of a foundation stone for a local hospital. This date was given over to commemorating Cabot, with parades, races, a ball, and fireworks, events that were organized by all-male committees. Cabot was also memorialized in a more permanent manner by the Cabot Tower in St. John's, a signal station built overlooking the harbour. While a debate was waged in the colony's press over the wisdom of spending funds on the tower (New-foundland had borne its share of the economic downturn of the 1890s), 5,000 people were attracted to the ceremony at which the tower's foundation stone was laid. As well as these events, the colony's government issued special stamps that featured both Cabot's arrival and Newfound-land's industrial and tourist attractions. While Cabot attracted far less attention in Canada, having to compete with figures such as Champlain and Cartier, the 1897 cel-ebrations appear to have helped solidify his image as rep-resentative of Newfoundland. When Newfoundland joined Confederation in 1949, its entry was marked by a com-memorative stamp that featured Cabot's ship, the *Matthew*.

Although many of these celebrations of the past took place in Atlantic Canada, Ontario, and Quebec, during these decades communities in the Prairie provinces also wished to remember the homelands that they had left in Britain or Europe and to leave a record of their particular groups' histories in Manitoba, Saskatchewan, and Alberta. Naming places – whether cities, rail stops, or colonies of newly arrived immigrants – after homes on the other side of the Atlantic was one way of linking older histories to a new identity in Canada; hence names such as Banff, Edmonton, Calgary, Islay, Icelandic River, Steinbach, and Altona dotted the Prairie map. These communities also created narratives of "founding fathers" who were instru-mental in bringing their members to Canada. Thus Sas-katchewan's Doukhobor community named the village of Verigin after Peter Verigin, the group's spiritual leader who came to Canada with his followers and whose leader-ship was remembered in pageants there during the 1940s and 1950s. Other sites – such as Saskatchewan's Hirsch, named after German-Jewish philanthropist Baron Mau-rice de Hirsch, or Esterhazy, called after the Hungarian immigration promoter Paul O. d'Esterhazy – memorialized those who had provided support in Europe for large-scale migration and settlement.

Such communities also provided sacred equivalents to the monuments built in eastern Canadian cities, as they founded churches that, whether Protestant, Catholic, or Orthodox, helped define the rural landscape as Christian space. They also provided vivid reminders of the communities' ethnic origins, being named after patron saints such as Elizabeth of Hungary, the Polish St. Stanislaus, or the Ukrainian saints Volodymyr and Olhe. Catholic immigrants also marked their homesteads with crosses and family shrines; these, along with pioneer graveyards, became the focus of pilgrimages during the interwar years that helped tie overseas origins to lives lived and communities created on the Canadian Prairies.

Like their counterparts in other Canadian communities engaged in public commemoration, these groups did not always agree on the narratives to be told, whether of their histories in Europe or in Canada. During the Depression, for example, socialists and communists within the Finnish, Jewish, and Ukrainian Prairie communities rejected narratives that depicted Canada as a "promised land," instead choosing to emphasize Canadian capitalism's exploitation of workers and the poverty and powerlessness suffered by Prairie farmers. However, overall the narratives told by these groups stressed their contributions to Canada through their settling the land and their struggles and sacrifice in this process; they also depicted themselves as embodying histories of perseverance, industry, thrift, religiosity, sobriety, and hospitality. While each group, whether Ukrainian, Scandinavian, Jewish, Icelandic, or Hungarian, claimed these qualities as the distinct properties of their respective communities, the similarity of these narratives also tended to suggest that Prairie immigrants shared a more homogenous identity.

As well as appearing in monuments and pageants, in the first few decades of the twentieth century, individuals and events from Canadian history were also memorialized in film. In 1913, Adam Dollard des Ormeaux's tale was made into a film, *The Battle of the Long Sault*, by the British American Film Company, which told the story as a thrilling clash between French soldiers and the Iroquois. In the 1920s, French-Canadian filmmakers realized the potential of Madeleine de Verchères's narrative, as her tale had dramatic action, a young female lead (an important aspect of movie-making in the period), and, with some expansion of the story's timeframe, could be given a romantic twist. Moreover, Verchères's story could be told in ways that meshed with French-Canadian Catholic values, thus helping to quell concerns about American cultural domination of Quebec (concerns that also were felt in English Canada, Britain, and France). Filmed in a custom-built fort at Kahnawake and featuring actors from Montreal and Kahnawake, *Madeleine de Verchères* opened in Montreal in December 1922 and went on to tour eighty-four parishes in Quebec, its story that of the youthful heroine's bravery and patriotic duty.

Five years later, the central organizing committee of the Diamond Jubilee of Confederation also believed that Canadians needed a grand celebration that would remake Dominion Day as a truly patriotic day, one which would promote a history of Canada organized around national themes. Led by Liberal prime minister William Lyon Mackenzie King, the Jubilee's Ottawa-based central organizing committee issued articles, monographs, booklets, and press releases on Canadian history; they also appeared on radio programs, using new technology to promote the past. The committee designed a wide range of public activities to inculcate national pride, such as civic processions, drum (military) tattoos, memorial ceremonies, outdoor concerts, historical pageants, community picnics, athletic competitions, and thanksgiving services. Unlike the Champlain Tercentenary, though, the Jubilee emphasized those historical events and developments that started in 1867, such as the British North America Act, lives of the Fathers of Confederation, developments in modern industrial growth, the spread of formal education, the completion of the Canadian Pacific Railway, and the First World War's Battle of Vimy Ridge (although they eventually ended up including Cartier, Champlain, and other early explorers). On 1 July, a large organized pageant was held in Ottawa, which featured thirty-one trucks bearing historic tableaux and several thousand costumed participants marching alongside.

However, while Canadians across the country enthusiastically took up the central committee's mandate to celebrate the Jubilee, local and provincial organizers did not always share their Ottawa counterparts' narratives of Canadian history. Pageants on the Prairies either depicted Western developments and figures, such as the arrival of the Royal Mounted North West Police and of Eastern Europeans, cowboys, and Western First Nations, without mentioning Cartier and Champlain. Winnipeg's celebrations made much of Ukrainian contributions to the city's history but said virtually nothing about a national narrative. In Montreal, despite the province's nationalist elites' desire to focus on the church's role and to glorify pre-industrial society and the habitant, the city's celebrations were more about progress and modernization of Quebec society, featuring its street railway, automobiles, and telephones. Toronto's 1 July celebrations featured a four-mile long pageant, with thirty-five floats, 8,000 marchers, and 120,000 spectators. Contrary to Ottawa's desire to commemorate the Fathers of Confederation, though, this display focused on the pre-Confederation period, starting with Indigenous people and including the arrival of Loyalists, the War of 1812, Egerton Ryerson, a Methodist camp meeting, and scenes from pioneer life. The participants depicted the post-1867 years with a veterans' float, added at the insistence of the local Legion, which featured survivors of the Fenian raids, the Northwest Rebellion, the Boer War, and the First World War.

Three groups decided to use the Jubilee festivities as an opportunity to claim their place in Canadian history: middle-class English-Canadian women, recent immigrants, and Indigenous people. Members of groups such as the National Council of Women and Imperial Order Daughters of the Empire (IODE) wrote numerous historical and religious scripts that were performed in hundreds of churches and schools across Canada. They also sat on local Jubilee committees; in some areas, such as the town of Welland in the Niagara peninsula, women's groups were entirely responsible for organizing Jubilee events. In Toronto, a local IODE chapter organized a large pageant at Massey Hall in which almost all the roles were played by women. The performance ran for three nights, all of which sold out. Immigrant communities, particularly in Winnipeg and across the Prairies, staged pageants that both affirmed their homeland identities – with clothing, music, and scenes from home countries' histories – and their commitment to Canada and assimilation to Canadian ways; the pageants customarily ended with both participants and audiences singing "O Canada," "The Maple Leaf Forever," and "God Save the King."

For their part, Aboriginal people insisted that they should participate in the Jubilee. They wrote to local Indian agents and the federal government, sending a stream of letters and petitions that requested both permission and funding for celebrations on their reserves. Although the Department of Indian Affairs initially refused their requests, they were overruled by the Ottawa organizing committee. It is not immediately obvious why Indigenous people should wish to join in celebrations of the nation that had subjected them to greater political and cultural control and coercion than any other Canadians and which, in 1927, revised the Indian Act to make it illegal to raise or grant funds for pursuit of Aboriginal land claims. Unlike newly enfranchised women or immigrants, Aboriginal people had little to gain from demonstrating patriotic pride or insisting that they belonged to Canada; by this point, for example, the members of the Six Nations had ceased to be active in the Ontario Historical Society (although in the 1930s and 1940s they played a leading role at the local level as members and officers of the Brant Historical Society). Furthermore, missionaries and government agents tried to ensure that their participation confirmed to the state's agenda of assimilation. At one western residential school, the pupils were made to enact scenes that depicted them throwing away their old way of life, including their "weird" spirituality, for Christian civilization; at St. Boniface, Manitoba, Aboriginal adults were given a script that ended with an Aboriginal chief offering to divide up land with whites provided that missionaries arrive and baptize them. As such examples suggest, many of these narratives were condescending and racist; they also suggested that Indigenous peoples' "history" only really began with the arrival of Europeans and their acceptance of white culture and Christianity. However, like their counterparts in 1908, Aboriginal peoples often "stole the show" and attracted tourists to fill the ranks of spectators. Moreover, in the Jubilee celebrations they seized opportunities to resurrect and display aspects of their culture – costumes, ceremonies, customs – that had been suppressed, doing so not just for non-Indigenous audiences but also for each other as a means of reviving and transmitting their histories.

These large-scale national or provincial pageants were not, of course, the only such events. One year after the Diamond Jubilee, residents of Kentville, Nova Scotia, staged a community pageant to commemorate the arrival of the province's "Planter" population, New Englanders who had arrived in 1760. Organized by members of the town's elite – local politicians, businessmen, and the editor of its newspaper – like its forerunners, the pageant was accompanied by other events, such as sports' competitions, fireworks, a beauty contest, and a parade. The dominant narrative of the pageant itself was that of the progress of the Planters' descendants, an important theme to stress, it seems, when communities across the Maritimes were losing residents to out-migration. Like previous celebrations, the Kentville pageant was marked by certain absences and exclusions:

Acadians were notable for their omission; the Mi'kmaq received only brief attention in the printed program and no historic Mi'kmaq figure appeared in the pageant; and United Empire Loyalists were also missing. The Kentville pageant had its fair share of female representation: it was directed by a woman, Daisy Foster, and out of the 400 participants, women played a majority of the roles, particularly as allegorical and iconic figures.

Yet although pageantry, like other forms of public history, was shaped by notions of who and what was historically significant and who was not, groups that had either been excluded from pageants or represented through stereotypes took up the form to present their own narratives. By the middle of the twentieth century, for example, Acadians in Nova Scotia used pageantry as a means of countering their absence from English-speaking celebrations, to celebrate their historical presence in the province, and to heal the wounds of both the *Grand Dérangement* (deportation) and their subsequent marginalization from Canadian society. In the mid-twentieth century, members of the Six Nations enacted pageants at the Grand River Reserve that told of their history in the Mohawk Valley, their historic alliance with Britain, and their arrival and settlement at the Grand River. Pageants were also staged in schools and by children's groups, such as the Boy Scouts and the Girl Guides, although fewer records that provide details about them appear to have survived (or at least they have not attracted the attention of many historians). Furthermore, pageants were often staged as part of local communities' "old home" or "homecoming" weeks, when towns organized festivities and invited former residents to "return home" to appreciate their own, and their community's, past. Such celebrations often were underpinned by their participants' desire to boost tourism and shore up local civic pride.

To be sure, as we have seen, pageants could present a very romanticized and disjointed narrative in which explanations for "why" things had occurred were never broached.

However, examining pageantry as a form of historical performance and knowledge demonstrates yet another venue in which people have sought to tell stories about their societies, displaying and using their bodies in material culture, song, dance, and display. Moreover, although monuments too had their shortcomings as a historical genre, since in late-Victorian and Edwardian Canada they tended to glorify only certain individuals (while then becoming so much of the landscape that they might be ignored), they were nevertheless meant to have a sacred and moving quality, to impart inspirational lessons that were as much about morality as they were historical. Both pageants and monuments thus might appeal to participants' and spectators' emotions and their senses, as well as having strong popular and public appeal.

The late nineteenth and early twentieth century, then, was a key period in which Canadians remembered their histories, one in which particular historical narratives were told in public and formal ways. Such forms of remembering were shaped by the context in which they took place, a context that included a range of factors. Cultural and intellectual concerns about Canada's status and the country's relationships with both Britain and the United States; the growth of the country's middle class; the expansion of both Confederation and the Dominion government's power; faster and wider-ranging transportation and communications networks that brought increased numbers of immigrants to Canada and, also, made it easier for like-minded individuals and groups to come together: all these elements combined to create a political, cultural, and social climate in which forming historical societies, building monuments, and staging pageants seemed not just important but necessary. As well, similar developments in both Britain and the United States helped provide both examples of models that might be followed and an impetus to claim a "history" for Canadians.

Of course, determining whether the commemorative events, societies, and edifices of the nineteenth and early twentieth centuries were successful in fulfilling their organizers' aspirations is difficult for historians. We cannot conduct surveys or interview people from this period to try to gauge the effectiveness of these commemorations and understand just what people took away from them. It is worth noting, though, that at times activists have used monuments to both remember *and* protest; in 1962, for example, the *Front de libération du Québec* bombed and decapitated the Queen Victoria statue in Quebec City, while John A. Macdonald's Montreal statue was beheaded in 1992. As well, the historical narratives and individuals featured in this period also formed the content of many school textbooks and historical readers, which suggests that the commemorators' work may have been influential outside of the discrete event of the pageant or the particular location of the monument. Furthermore, the realms of the emotions and the senses that so many late-Victorian and Edwardian commemorators drew upon would play important roles in remembering – and forgetting – the histories of Canada's participation in war and military conflict.

4

Remembering Canada at War

War, both civil and between nations, has probably been one of the historical events most remembered by nineteenth- and twentieth-century commemorators; monuments, poetry, drama, novels, song, paintings, and other genres have memorialized battles and individuals, ranging from the well-known generals of the Napoleonic Wars to the Unknown Soldier of the First World War. Such a pattern of remembering war continues today, as witnessed by the popularity of books on military history, the ubiquity of programs devoted to war on the History Channel, and commemorations of the War of 1812. To be sure, at times current wars and the memory of past ones have been the focus of condemnation, not commemoration, such as the 1950s anti-nuclear movement and the 1960s and 1970s international campaign against the war in Southeast Asia. Nevertheless, military conflict has often been a central preoccupation of commemorators.

Determining why this has been the case is not an easy task, since particular historical contexts – the specificities of time and place – influence when, where, to whom, and why certain forms of remembering took place. It is possible, though, to suggest a few explanations for war's popularity among commemorators. For one, those who created historical narratives and representations often wished as well to create national identities and reinforce the boundaries of nations, the latter often shaped in the nineteenth and twentieth centuries through armed conflict. Rather than war being perceived as a tragedy to be avoided and its memory ignored, these groups often saw it as a central force in forging nations and providing examples of valour for future citizens to remember and emulate. As well, society's attitude towards the military changed. The image of the army altered over the course of the nineteenth century; perceptions of soldiers as dangerous and potentially threatening to civilian order shifted somewhat to encompass the notion of the soldier as self-sacrificing, noble, and heroic. Participating in military conflicts also became an important part of asserting one's right to participate in civil life, politically, socially, and economically. Furthermore, for those who had lost family and friends in large-scale wars that involved volunteer forces, such as the First World War, memorializing both the soldiers and the war itself might help to assuage grief and provide meaning for the losses suffered.

The War of 1812 received its fair share of attention, particularly in Ontario and particularly in the late nineteenth and early twentieth century. However, British North Americans were from time to time drawn in by conflicts fought on international soil that, like the War of 1812, were part of larger, global struggles. While British North America's involvement in the Crimean War of the 1850s was not extensive, Halifax dedicated its first public monument to two young men killed in the Crimea in 1855. In 1860, a thirty-foot memorial, topped with a large lion and bearing the soldiers' names, "Parker" and "Welsford," along with the names of Crimean battles (Alma, Redan, Inkerman, Balaclava, and Sebastopol), was installed with the assistance of the local garrison. Eight years later, volunteers in French-Catholic Quebec were encouraged to defend papal territory in Italy. The Papal Zouaves, as the regiment was known, were memorialized in Valleyfield, south of Montreal, as well as in the Eastern Township community of Marston-Sud, where many returning veterans settled. Their parish,

Piopolis, was named after Pope Pius IX, and Marston-Sud was renamed Piopolis in 1958.

Conflicts closer to home, too, were marked by the building of monuments and their public dedication ceremonies. In 1866, the Fenian Brotherhood, an Irish-American organization which called for Ireland's independence from British colonial rule, staged raids into New Brunswick, Quebec, and Ontario, thereby hoping to pressure the British government into withdrawal from Ireland. The raids were defeated, although not without the deaths of a number of Canadians at Ridgeway, a town in the Niagara peninsula not far from Fort Erie. One year after the raids, Alexander Muir, who served against the Fenians in the Battle of Ridgeway, wrote "The Maple Leaf Forever," a song which appeals to the Britishness of Canadian history and which would become an unofficial anthem for English Canada. Other tributes to the defeat of the Fenians followed. In 1870, four years after the raids and three years after Confederation, the city of Toronto put up a monument to those who had died – either in battle or from disease – opposing the Fenians. Built with subscriptions sent from across the province and donors from Quebec, the monument's inscription celebrated the militia members as being of "the people," and its designer, Robert Reid, included a number of allegorical and military figures. Three of those killed were students from the University of Toronto; they, too, were remembered on its campus with a stained-glass window in University College's Upper East Hall.

While the Crimea and Zouave campaigns had particular meanings for those directly involved – contributing to Britain's imperial position and shoring up ultramontane devotion in Quebec – and the Fenian raids have been said to have contributed to Confederation, the Northwest Rebellion of 1885 was a pivotal conflict, one that took place on "Canadian" terrain and that had far-reaching political, social, and cultural implications. The suppression of the Metis' and First Nations' uprising by armed militias from the Maritimes, Quebec, Ontario, and Winnipeg became the subject of a number of monuments, particularly in Ontario where support for the government's actions was often clearly voiced. In Port Hope, on Lake Ontario between Toronto and Kingston, a statue of Lieutenant-Colonel Arthur T.H. Williams was unveiled in September 1889; the ceremony was attended by John A. Macdonald and timed to coincide with the first day of the town's Industrial Exhibition. Williams, the local MP and battalion commander for eastern Ontario, had led his troops at the Battle of Batoche, an action that went against the orders of his commander, British General Frederick Middleton, but that has been seen by historians as having brought a quick resolution in the government's favour. Although Williams was not killed in battle but had died of disease, the monument shows him wielding his sword as he leads his troops. The monument's inscription calls for Canadians to remember Williams's "devoted patriotism and heroic bravery," words which would prove prescient after the First World War. In Ontario, the Port Hope statue was followed by monuments in St. Catharines, Ottawa, Queen's Park in Toronto, and Peterborough, and in Russell, Manitoba. Two white women caught up in the events also published narratives of their supposed terrifying "captivity" by Big Bear and the Metis; it is more than likely, though, that they were taken into Big Bear's camp for protection and were free to leave at any time. However, their stories of the events of 1885 built on earlier captivity narratives published in the United States, ones that a number of English Canadians might have encountered as part of religious and popular reading and which contributed to images of Aboriginal and Metis men as savages who threatened white women's virtue.

As we shall see, the memorialization of Louis Riel and Aboriginal leaders such as Big Bear also occurred in a number of genres: statues, historic sites, fiction, poetry, opera, theatre, television, and film. However, generally these forms of memory were created later in the twentieth century and at times were the subject of considerable public controversy.

Other conflicts, such as the South African War, were also met with public enthusiasm and support in English-speaking Canada. To be sure, the war in South Africa between the British and Dutch settlers was an imperial one, having little direct bearing on either Canadian or even British sovereignty. Nevertheless, it took place in a context of growing support for the British Empire, both in Canada and internationally. Such support was bolstered by widespread notions of the superiority of the Anglo-Saxon "race," a desire for Canada to prove her loyalty as a semi-autonomous Dominion, and a greater interest in the Canadian military. Although Canada's combined contingents of 8,400 troops fell far behind those sent by Australia (16,500), and the war effort was met with strong opposition by Quebec nationalists, celebratory commemorations of the war nonetheless began to take shape even before it ended. As the troops boarded ships bound for South Africa, the English-Canadian public deluged retailers with demands for commemorative and souvenir items, such as postcards, books, maps, buttons; commemorative plates and khaki handkerchiefs and suspenders became "must-have" items for the patriotic. A raft of new charitable organizations provided support for soldiers and their dependents and, in 1900, prominent citizens of Victoria and Montreal organized committees to put up memorials.

At the war's end, Canadians wasted little time in memorializing those who had fought, as portraits, busts, tablets, and monuments were put up in places such as Port Hope, Winnipeg, Amherst Island, and the Royal Canadian Military College in Ontario, Calgary in Alberta, Granby in Quebec, and McGill University in Montreal. Along with the Victoria, Quebec, and Montreal memorials, patriotic organizations marked the public spaces of cities, towns, and villages, such as Ottawa, Halifax, Charlottetown, Toronto, Brantford, Sarnia, Newmarket, and Southampton, with statues by sculptors such as Hamilton McCarthy, Louis-Philippe Hébert, and Walter Allward, memorials which called attention to Canada's contribution to the imperial cause. Local newspapers were eager to cover the campaigns and fundraising efforts for South African War monuments, publishing lists of subscribers, proposed designs, and letters to the chairs of the various committees.

Not all of these efforts went smoothly or were without conflict. In London, disputes erupted into the public eye between two factions of the city's Imperial Order Daughters of the Empire (IODE) chapter, a recently founded organization focused on promoting Canadian patriotism and ties to the Empire. The IODE had been fundraising for a soldiers' memorial approved by the city's council and had collected $10,000, primarily from schoolchildren's donations and concerts. However, some members of the organization also wished to include the recently deceased Queen Victoria with a plaque on the memorial, a suggestion that other members saw as disrespectful to the late monarch's memory. After the disagreement made the pages of the local press and became increasingly heated, with members casting aspersions on the loyalty of their opponents, the national organization expelled the chapter and a group of local businessmen decided the monument's fate. When completed, the memorial featured a woman offering a laurel crown to a soldier marching above her. Whether she represents Victoria is left up to the viewer.

Territorial disputes marked other efforts to memorializing Canada's contribution to the South African War. The Canadian South African Memorial Association, formed in 1902 by Lady Minto, the governor general's wife, the minister of the militia, and other prominent figures, aimed at identifying and marking the grave sites of the 270 Canadians who died in South Africa. Here again the IODE was involved, since in 1901 they had offered to help the South African Graves Fund do similar work and saw the Association as offering needless competition. Although Lady Minto was the IODE's official patron and attempted to bring the two groups together, the two groups competed with each other to honour the dead. In the end, the Association, with its network of well-off and influential contacts in Canada and South Africa, won out. By 1909, over $14,000 had been raised for 180 granite memorials that were shipped to South Africa and installed. The graves were cared for by the Guild of Loyal Women of South Africa, supported by the Association and, later, the IODE.

The memory of the South African War did not end with monuments, though. Veterans also relived their experiences through dinners, company reunions, South African Veterans' Association meetings, and the South African Medals Association; they also created memories in more intimate ways by revisiting scrapbooks, collections of photography, and talking among themselves. As well, various levels of the Canadian government remembered their contribution to the imperial cause, as it offered the veterans land grants of 160 acres in Northwest Canada. Two hundred of them represented Canada at Edward VII's coronation, while others were able to parlay their South African War service into public office or military positions of higher rank. Some soldiers became public lecturers on their return to Canada, speaking about their experiences in South Africa. At a more abstract level, the memory of the South African War underpinned debates over imperialism, pro or con, especially within Quebec, and over the issue of conscription. It also helped raise the visibility and status of the Canadian militia; the latter's wartime work helped legitimate arguments to increase its size, funding, level of training, and equipment. Like the myth of the loyal militia of 1812 – which was created long before the South African War and elaborated during the early twentieth century – narratives of the militia's importance were used to argue for a trained force of citizens, not a standing army. All this occurred even though such narratives irritated British officials who felt that Canadians' confidence in their military importance, not to mention criticism of British strategies and organization, was unjust and unwarranted.

The First World War would lead to nationwide commemorations of Canada's military on an even larger scale and in multiple genres. Some Canadians had commemoration on their minds not long after the war broke out. After all, historical commemoration and the construction of collective memory had become a central preoccupation for a number of middle-class Canadians in both French and English Canada; as well, calls to remember both the Northwest Rebellion and the South African War may also have provided inspiration and motivation. Whatever the case, in December 1914, four months after the first shots were fired and before many Canadian troops had reached Europe, Vancouver's Canadian Club asked the provincial government to designate the city's old Court House Square for a memorial. Other requests for such spaces were to follow: the Belleville, Ontario, Women's Red Cross asked Ottawa for land in front of the city's armories; a temporary monument was built on British Columbia's Saltspring Island; and the sculptor Frances Loring built a large temporary monument, "Canada Sending Her Sons to War," at Toronto's Canadian National Exhibition. At least one granite company saw potential business opportunities for itself after the war's end. In April 1917, Middleton and Eastman, a granite merchant based in Hamilton, asked army headquarters for help with technical details; responding to customer demand, they were getting ready to produce statues and wanted their representations to be accurate.

After the war, though, creating a memory both of the war itself and those Canadians who had served in it became almost an obsession for many Canadians. Throughout the 1920s and 1930s, Canadians worked hard to commemorate the "Great War" in a number of ways that were multifaceted in the genres that they took but remarkably similar in their thematic and didactic unity. One of the most publicly visible means of commemorating the First World War, though, which survives to the present day, was the war memorial; these statues, obelisks, and shafts became so ubiquitous that one can still be found in almost every small town in English Canada. Although a number of well-known writers and intellectuals in Britain, as well as pacifist movements in Canada, Britain, and the United States, believed the war to have been a tragic and pointless exercise that should be mourned, not celebrated, public representations in Canada (and elsewhere) depicted the First World War quite differently. The monuments unveiled in cities, towns, and villages tended to portray the war and those who fought it as embodying a glorious triumph of Canadian manhood, not a deplorable loss. Many of these statues and monuments, moreover, celebrated not just Canadian officers but, rather, the ordinary Canadian soldier, a theme that would emerge in veterans' reunions and Remembrance Day ceremonies. This soldier, far from being brutalized or traumatized by his experiences, was an inspirational, Christ-like figure who willingly, one might even say joyfully, sacrificed himself for his country and home (in many ways resembling the images and narratives of General Brock's sacrifice at Queenston Heights). Such a commemoration was underscored by the fact that the monuments listed the names of the dead, a memorialization that tied the soldiers directly to their communities. It also would prove important in perpetuating that memory, providing a direct reminder for participants in Remembrance Day ceremonies and those who made their own private, less formal visits to the cenotaph of those who sacrificed themselves for community and nation (and, equally importantly, those who had not).

To be sure, not all of these memorials took the form of the Christian soldier. The First World War monument in Trois-Rivières shows not a Christ-like figure but, instead, a soldier in the act of thrusting his bayonet into an invisible enemy, an image that reminded onlookers of the physical aggression and violence needed even in the commission of a "just war." Furthermore, the statue in the upper-class

Montreal suburb of Outremont is that of an allegorical woman who mourns for the war dead; she might be a mother, wife, sister, or even Canada personified as a woman. Here male heroism takes a back seat to the terrible losses sustained during the war. Thus, even though the bulk of the monuments helped to shape a public, collective memory of the events of 1914–18 that depicted the war as a noble and dignified endeavour, at times communities decided to represent the war in rather different terms.

Moreover, although the First World War has been seen as a particularly "modern" war, emblematic – even prophetic – of twentieth-century warfare in the technology used to fight it, the ways in which it was remembered in Canada drew very much upon the conventions, genres, imagery, and symbolism used to commemorate the War of 1812, the Northwest Rebellion, and the South African War. Tanks or other forms of new weaponry did not figure in either the monuments or in other forms of visual representations, such as paintings. Even images of aviators, who had started to appear in the European theatre and were most definitely exemplary of modern technology, shied away from the technical and mechanized aspects of flight. They were not depicted as being able to kill from a distance and thus be part of a newer, dehumanized approach to warfare – an image that, for example, emerged during the Spanish Civil War in Pablo Picasso's famous 1937 painting *Guernica*. Rather, they were seen as chivalrous knights of the air, free from the drudgery and dirt of trench warfare.

As well as tributes in stone, stained-glass, canvas, and text, the First World War was remembered in public ceremonies held on Armistice Day or, as Canadians came to know it, Remembrance Day. Following the passage of Dominion government legislation in 1921, Armistice Day was held on the Monday of the week of November 11, the day that marked the official end of the war (and which was also Canadian Thanksgiving). Over the course of the 1920s, churches held ceremonies and veterans gathered at town cenotaphs without much overt controversy. However, by the end of the decade, Canadians began to debate the nature of Armistice Day, asking whether remembering the events of 1914–18 warranted a separate day and, too, whether the war should be considered a celebration of past military triumph or as a means of ensuring future peace. In 1931, government legislation renamed Armistice Day to Remembrance Day, and changed the date of Thanksgiving, so that Canadians could now remember the war with its own, separate day. Nevertheless, the question of the tone of the services was not so easily resolved. Although services on Remembrance Day might call for future peace, the war itself was remembered as a noble and necessary sacrifice, not as a tragedy or as a reminder of the futility of armed conflict between nations.

In addition to attending large-scale public ceremonies on 11 November, Canadians also might travel overseas to visit battlefields and war graves, trips that became known as pilgrimages. By 1919, visiting battlefields had a long history among Europeans, British, and North American commemorators and tourists, whether the site in question was Waterloo, civil war sites, or Queenston Heights. In the context of the First World War, tourists began arriving on an informal basis at French and Belgian battlefields almost when hostilities had ended, a traffic which continued throughout the 1920s and into the 1930s. As the British and Dominion governments had agreed with the Imperial War Graves Commission's decision to leave the war dead in Europe and maintain cemeteries, with well-tended paths and (where possible) clearly marked graves, a number of Canadians made the trip overseas to visit a loved one's resting place. Individuals might organize their trips on a personal and informal level, evoking and reliving intimate memories of the war. Such was the case of Effie Laurie Storer, a Saskatchewan journalist who, in 1923, went to tour French battlefields and visit her husband's grave and that of her friend's husband. Storer was pleased by what she found, writing to her friends at home that her husband was in a "lovely spot," very pretty and peaceful.[1] She also noted the many other women who, accompanied by sons who had been too young to enlist, were searching for their elder sons' graves.

Besides travellers such as Storer, other Canadians travelled to First World War battlefields as part of more highly visible, formally organized pilgrimages, such as the 1936 trip by veterans to witness the unveiling of the Vimy Ridge monument in France. Attended by 6,000 Canadians, veterans from England, Scotland, Ireland, Australia, and, according to one Canadian observer, Morocco also made the pilgrimage. A few Canadians left accounts of their experiences. John Risser, a commercial traveller from Nova Scotia's Lunenburg County, sent back columns to a Bridgewater newspaper. While he appreciated the warm welcome he and his fellow Canadians received in France, he noted that the organization of the cemetery tours was disappointing; people got into the wrong cars, their drivers were unable to speak English and were lost, and those who went to Thiepval Monument were caught in a thunderstorm and were soaked. His account of the Vimy monument's dedication ceremony is fairly matter-of-fact. Risser recounted the number of souvenir sellers who lined the road, the order and length of the service, the number of airplanes which flew by and the wreaths laid, and that it was quite hot and a number of men had to be carried off on stretchers. Like a number of his fellow pilgrims, Risser spent some time in Britain where, on a Thames boat trip, he met two young men from Germany, crew members on a ship from Hamburg. "They were non-committal about conditions in Germany and did not like it when we questioned them about Hitler, only to say 'he was a good man.' They highly resented the opinions we had of Hitler."[2] He also heard a speaker

---

1 Effie Laurie Storer, Travel Diary 1923, 11 July 1923, Effie Laurie Storer Papers, S-A 186 1.2 and 3, Public Archives of Saskatchewan (Saskatoon).
2 John Risser, "Scrapbook: Notes on Vimy Memorial Pilgrimage Tour, by a Member of the Party," 3 Sept. 1936, MS 1791, Public Archives of Nova Scotia.

in Trafalgar Square praising Benito Mussolini and saw him
giving the "Fascist salute" which, Risser noted, was acknowledged enthusiastically by some members of the crowd.
If Risser's account said more about the details of the ceremony and told his readers about the present state of affairs
in Europe, then fellow Nova Scotian Frank Ferguson, who
left an unpublished account of his trip, was by turns mock-
ing and reverential in his attitude towards the war and the
ceremonies. Ferguson thought "it was a grand sight to see
the parade of ships sailing down the river (out of Montreal
harbour) headed for France bearing back to the scene of
their 'crimes' so many men who twenty years ago would have
gladly given all they possessed to be some other place."[3]
Once in France, Ferguson saw both familiar spots but also
many changes: "What seemed to me as being most wonderful was the complete lack of MUD." To him, the monument
to the South African troops was quite wonderful but he was
unimpressed by the British War Memorial at Thiepval: "To
my mind it resembles nothing more than a big apartment
house standing there waiting for the tenants to move in."
Once he reached the Vimy monument, his tone changed:

As one approaches the monument he is struck by its tremendous
size and ... its tall tapering pylons reaching high into the sun, and
the white clouds which formed a background for this wonderful
structure, when first I saw it seemed almost to have been set for
the occasion. I will not dwell on the subject of this most wonderful of monuments, erected to the memory of those brave lads who
"went over the hump" and did not return, as that has been done
so well by others more versed in the description of such things. As
far as the Ceremony goes all I can say it was the most impressive
thing I have ever witnessed, and it was with great pride I stood
out in front of this beautiful thing of stone to hear from the lips
of that brown haired lad, His Majesty the King of all Englishmen,

---

3 Frank Byron Ferguson, "One 'Old Soldier' Went Back! Or Eighteen Years
   Later," 13, 1918–1936, MS-2-285.A.3, Dalhousie University Archives.

these words. "For this glorious monument crowning the hill of Vimy, is now and for all time part of Canada."[4]

Constructs of gender relations helped shape the images and representations of the war. Masculinity was a central characteristic; Canadian men and Canadian manhood featured most prominently in the First World War's commemoration. While it might seem obvious that this would be the case, given that women were excluded from combat and Canada suffered a high rate of male casualties, commemorative practices and images linked masculinity, wartime service, and nationality very directly and clearly. Just as the militia of the War of 1812 or the troops sent to the Northwest in 1885 were seen as exemplifying Canadian manhood, so too did the soldiers of the Canadian Expeditionary Force (CEF) personify the best qualities of the "new" Canadian nation. They were vigorous, courageous, morally upright, youthful, and, especially important, they represented particular areas of Canada: its farms, fisheries, and forests. Although the vast majority of the CEF were from urban areas and small towns and were just as likely to be bank clerks and factory workers as fishermen and lumberjacks, poetry, fiction, speeches, and other forms of public remembrance depicted Canadian soldiers as products of unspoiled, natural settings that, in turn, exemplified the Canadian nation in their purity. Moreover, while Canadian women had provided formal and informal support on the home front, and had been the recipients of government propaganda telling them of its great value to the war effort, their contributions received far fewer tributes (as was the case for much of the public commemorations of Loyalism and 1812).

However, many commemorative efforts, particularly fundraising for monuments, were spearheaded and run by

---

4 Ibid., 20–1.

women's organizations, such as the IODE, the Women's Institute, the Women's Christian Temperance Union, and local Councils of Women, as well as patriotic and Lest We Forget Societies. As well, a group of Canadian women were instrumental in erecting one of the very few memorials to women's wartime service. In August 1926, the Canadian Nurses' Association War Memorial was unveiled in Ottawa, on Parliament Hill's Centre Block. A tribute to the forty-nine Canadian nurses killed in the First World War, the memorial presented a particular version of women's nursing history in Canada, stretching from the nuns of New France to those who had just served overseas. As well as the more generic nurses remembered in the memorial, the British nurse Edith Cavell, executed by the Germans in 1915 for helping British prisoners escape from occupied Belgium, received a number of tributes in Canada. Cavell's story spread rapidly around the Empire shortly after her death and was used by British propagandists as a means to further depict the enemy as subhuman, brutal, and depraved. Like the Christian soldier, Cavell was depicted as a martyr, courageous and self-sacrificing, who, despite her physical weakness because of her sex, provided an example of courage and stoicism. Although Cavell nursed soldiers from both sides, refused to express hatred of the Germans, and told her chaplain on the evening before her execution that "patriotism is not enough,"[5] these aspects of her life were ignored in a rush to create a symbol that would rally civilians and troops (indeed, enlistment in Britain rose from 5,000 per week just before her death to 10,000 for eight weeks after it). In Canada, Cavell was publicly remembered first in 1916 by the naming of a mountain in Jasper National Park, officially dedicated in 1921, and then in 1919 with a bronze sculpture, created by Florence Wyle and placed on the grounds

---

5   Katie Pickles, *Transnational Outrage: The Death and Commemoration of Edith Cavell* (Hampshire, UK: Palgrave Macmillan, 2007), 40.

of Toronto General Hospital (not to be outdone, Toronto Western Hospital featured the Edith Cavell Wing). Schools in Moncton, St. Catharines, Sault Ste. Marie, Windsor, and Vancouver were named after Cavell, as well as Belleville's Edith Cavell Regional School of Nursing. Canadians living in Winnipeg, Port Stanley, Toronto, and Guelph also might be reminded of her memory as they walked or drove down Edith Cavell Avenue, Boulevard, or Drive. In 1930, the Canadian Post Office issued a $1.00 stamp that depicted Mount Edith Cavell, although its expense probably limited its exposure to a smaller group of better-off Canadians.

As well as nurses, women's role as mothers of soldiers killed in the war received official commemorative status. Although originally intended for the wives and mothers who had lost husbands and sons, the Memorial Cross medal, struck 1 December 1919 by the Privy Council, became associated primarily with the latter. During the war, a number of Canadian writers called on the Dominion government to recognize mothers' sacrifices and loss. William Alexander Fraser, for example, thought that a small silver cross would be appropriate, and a Mothers' Recognition Committee was formed in London, Ontario, to ensure that the mothers' gift of their sons to the nation was honoured (and that the sons' valour and heroism was also remembered). A number of stories emerged in the English-Canadian press, both during and especially after the war, of such women; in August 1920, an open-air car appeared in a veterans' parade, carrying four mothers who had seen, in total, twenty-eight sons die.

As part of the Vimy Ridge pilgrimage, Winnipeg's Mrs. Charlotte Susan Wood was introduced to King Edward VII as the first Silver Cross Mother and laid a wreath on Westminster Abbey's Tomb of the Unknown Warrior; eleven of Mrs. Wood's twelve sons had enlisted and five had been killed. In that ceremony, Wood was accompanied by British Columbia's Eleanor Garrard Watson, whose son's body had not been found. In her journal, Watson observed that "the

French government are flabbergasted ... that over 4,000 have accepted the invitations to France, they meant it for the ex-service men and their wives, and widows and mothers who had lost their sons and all sorts of people have seized the chance of a tour." She found the monument "too wonderful for words." When the cord was pulled and the Union Jack that covered it fell away, it revealed a figure of a veiled woman, head bowed, "sorrowing for her children. It is an incredibly beautiful figure ... Few of the men were dry-eyed. They were recalling the viewing that ridge as they remembered it, a mass of barbed wire, a sea of mud and blood."[6] Watson walked around the monument until she found her son Hamish's name carved on it. At the Tomb of the Unknown Soldier in Westminster Abbey, Watson was moved by "a wonderful feeling and I suppose each of us thought that 'he' may have been our dear 'missing one.'"[7] During the Second World War, Silver Cross Mothers started to occupy more prominent positions at Remembrance Day ceremonies; for example, the Royal Canadian Legion began the practice of choosing one Silver Cross Mother to represent all of her peers in Ottawa at the Cenotaph on 11 November.

We might justly ask why Canadians commemorated the war in this manner. After all, a number of prominent writers – particularly in Britain but also in Canada and Australia – left records of the First World War's hideousness: the filth and general misery of the trenches, the horrors of new weapons, such as mustard and chlorine gas, and the incompetence of generals. Why, then, weren't there more public denunciations of war, condemnations of the toll it had taken on Canada (not to mention Europe and Britain)? Why was there so little scepticism, even cynicism, expressed in the face of commemorations that focused so relentlessly on the First World War as a noble

6 Eleanor Garrard Watson, Travel Diary 1936, 26 July 1936, Box 1, MS830, Garrard Family Papers, Archives of British Columbia.
7 Ibid., 29 July 1936.

and worthy sacrifice? Historians have attempted to grapple with these questions. For one, the sheer scale of death warranted some kind of collective myth or narrative to provide solace in the face of so many dead. As well, these ways of commemorating the First World War were not just created by elites or the government. Many Canadians participated in crafting these representations of the war; the government often lagged behind or was not directly involved in efforts to commemorate the dead. After all, for the vast majority of Canadians, the number of war dead – 53,000 in trench warfare alone – was an unprecedented loss of male family members, friends, and acquaintances in a military conflict.

The concept of the war as glorious and noble was also meant to unify a nation that had been riven by the debates over conscription. Some Canadians, both French and, in particular, English, felt that there was a wound in Canada's national consciousness that needed to be healed (not unlike commemorations of the U.S. Civil War). Moreover, the 1920s were a turbulent decade, especially in the war's immediate aftermath; they did not "boom" for everyone, particularly those veterans whose return home left them with feelings of abandonment. For some of those men, participating in veterans' reunions, Remembrance Day ceremonies, and the Vimy pilgrimage might help assuage their disappointment. The myth of the war was also meant to bring together new Canadians, especially Eastern European immigrants, and to assure Indigenous Canadians, who per capita had been one of the largest communities to volunteer, that they too were part of the Canadian nation. For some political leaders, such an assurance was quite important in the face of the nascent Indigenous rights movement of the 1920s, spearheaded by the returned veteran and Mohawk leader Onondeyoh (Frederick Loft).

Furthermore, the narrative of the First World War as a glorious sacrifice was not unique to Canada. In Newfoundland, both unofficial and official memories of the First Battalion of the Newfoundland regiment's experiences at Gallipoli in Turkey (April 1915–January 1916) and Beaumont Hamel in France (1 July 1916) played important roles in sustaining Newfoundland nationalism and support for the colony's tie to Britain. At Gallipoli, the Battalion endured heat, flies, shortages of food and water, and periods of boredom; they also, though, lost over 700 men (out of a total of 900) as a result of disease, artillery fire, and snipers. While the authorities deemed the evacuation of Gallipoli a military success, one in which the Newfoundlanders played an important role, their experiences were far from the excitement of combat that many of the young men expected. However, both during the event and in the interwar decades, Newfoundlanders remembered Gallipoli as a significant test of the regiment's – and by extension, the colony's – ability to serve both Newfoundland and Empire with stoicism, reliability, and Christian self-sacrifice. That the enemy they faced at Gallipoli was Turkey also led some commemorators to depict the conflict as a crusade against "the infidel." During the war, soldiers' letters home emphasized such themes, as did official accounts of Gallipoli that praised the troops' fortitude (and called for more volunteers), and the casualty lists that included glowing tributes to the fallen. In the interwar years, soldiers' diaries and memoirs, along with letters to the island's newspapers and articles that recounted the regiment's self-sacrifices, regimental histories, public presentations, and fiction all contributed to a picture of Gallipoli that admitted conditions were atrocious. They also stressed, though, that Newfoundlanders' determination and dedication to a larger cause distinguished their service. Interestingly enough, the bitterness and anger that some members of the Australian and New Zealand Army Corps demonstrated towards Britain for mismanagement of the Gallipoli Campaign – emotions which helped feed nascent nationalism in Australia – was not displayed by their Newfoundland counterparts. Instead, they interpreted the events in Turkey as a worthy sacrifice for the imperial effort.

Such an interpretation also dominated the events of 1 July 1916, when at Beaumont Hamel in France the First Battalion's advance on German troops resulted in widespread losses, ones sustained without the former having fired a shot (out of 800 men, 233 were killed and 477 were wounded or missing). Despite this, though, Beaumont Hamel was remembered in a romantic and optimistic manner; it, too, was seen as an example of Christian devotion and patriotic dedication, a memory formed in its immediate aftermath. At the time, this memory served pressing practical realities, since Newfoundland military authorities wished to shore up recruitment in the face of the regiment's almost complete decimation and ensure that Britain did not take it out of combat. Over the war's duration and into the interwar years, Beaumont Hamel came to symbolize a new standard of courage and discipline, one that could be broadened to include all Newfoundlanders. In 1918, 1 July became the colony's official day of remembrance, one marked by the state, churches, and press as one in which Newfoundlanders might band together. Civilians who had not fought, for example, might honour the colony's efforts through acts of selflessness: helping veterans and the families of the war dead, for example, or teaching children about the mythic legacy of the First World War. In 1925, after a fund-raising campaign and contributions by the colony's government, the Beaumont Hamel Memorial Park was opened on the battlefield's site. Featuring a main sculpture of an oversized bronze caribou (which appeared on the Battalion's emblem) on top of a granite mound, its head arched as if, one spectator thought, issuing a call to battle, the park also maintained the original marks the battle had left on the land. Visitors thus might feel they were entering a space dedicated both to the solemnity of war and to Newfoundlanders' triumphal sacrifice for their homeland and Empire. The latter's significance was emphasized in the unveiling ceremony: the sculpture was covered with a Union Jack removed by British Field Marshal Alexander

Haig. The Beaumont Hamel Park, though, was also seen by the Newfoundland government as a way of promoting the colony during a period of political and economic turmoil. To be sure, such attempts to draw everyone into the nation through the First World War commemoration were not entirely successful. French Canadians did not forget the vicious attacks, both inside and outside Parliament, that had been mounted on them in the conscription debates. Furthermore, they also expressed their own ideas of Canada and of Quebec in statues and memorials put up for individuals such as Champlain and Cartier. Ukrainian-Canadians also had an ambivalent perspective on the war, since members of that group had been interned as enemy aliens and stripped of their citizenship. Such treatment, therefore, made it particularly important to this community that their contributions to Prairie settlement and voluntary military service be recognized and respected. In Newfoundland, both the government and many Newfoundlanders worked hard to promote the memory of wartime participation as emblematic of the strength of Newfoundland nationalism and imperial dedication, an inspiration that would help the colony's residents deal with the difficulties they experienced in the 1930s and 1940s. However, such memories were not enough to prevent the loss of Newfoundland's sovereignty in 1934, or the 1949 decision to join Canadian Confederation. After those events, the memory of Beaumont Hamel shifted to a more tragic one – the beginning of a long decline in Newfoundland's fortunes. As a result, 1 July, which in Canada was Dominion Day, was seen not as a day of celebration of Newfoundlanders' bravery but, rather, as a day of mourning.

French Canadians and Newfoundlanders were not alone in such experiences. Despite Aboriginal Canadians' records of wartime valour, Aboriginal veterans continued to face political and socio-economic discrimination. The government discriminated against them in the Soldiers' Settlements they received and, furthermore, Aboriginal people remained disfranchised (conversely, the Department of Indian Affairs attempted to enfranchise certain Indigenous leaders, such as Onondeyoh, in an attempt to remove them from their communities). This does not mean, of course, that Aboriginal communities forgot their members' service or that their leaders were not proud of men such as Francis Pegahmagabow, the Ojibwa army sniper who earned a number of medals in the First World War. Pegahmagabow was inducted into the Indian Hall of Fame at the Woodland Centre at the Six Nations reserve near Brantford, Ontario. As well, a plaque which commemorates him and his regiment was put up on the Rotary and Algonquin Regiment Fitness Trail in Parry Sound; the Canadian Forces named a building at Camp Borden after him; and, in 2005, Metis novelist Joseph Boyden used Pegahmagabow and his story in his award-winning novel, *Three Day Road*. Yet, for the most part, the Canadian government and general public have only recently acknowledged and honoured Aboriginal veterans' service and contributions to the First and Second World Wars, as well as the Korean War.

Japanese-Canadian veterans did not fare much better. The case of the decorated First World War veteran Sergeant Masumi Mitsui and the Vancouver Japanese-Canadian War Memorial shows how a particular context might come to overshadow, almost eliminate, previous commemorations of an individual and his community. At the end of the First World War, the Japanese-Canadian community organized fundraising for a new war memorial in Vancouver. The city rewarded their efforts with a site in Stanley Park; the memorial combined both Western and Japanese influences and featured plaques that listed both fallen soldiers from the community and returning veterans. The ceremony dedicating the monument was intended both to remember the soldiers' contributions and to call for the enfranchisement of Japanese-Canadians. In 1931, their struggle at the provincial level successful, a group of veterans met again at the monument, both to remember the veterans and celebrate.

Yet with the outbreak of the Second World War and the federal government's internment and forced removal of Japanese-Canadians from the lower mainland, the Japanese-Canadian War Memorial was no longer the scene of Remembrance Day or any other types of celebrations; the lantern at the memorial was extinguished. Not until 1985, when the treatment of Japanese-Canadians was understood as discriminatory and unjust, did Sergeant Mitsui return to the memorial (he, too, had been removed from Vancouver) for a re-lighting ceremony which, for him, meant remembering fallen comrades.

So far as formal monuments were concerned, the Second World War and the Korean War were often remembered not by separate memorials – although those were erected – but, more frequently, by the addition of veterans' names to existing First World War monuments. It is possible that the much smaller number of Canadians who died in the Second World War was the reason for this practice; higher casualty rates might have led to communities building separate monuments. A separate memorial to Canadian veterans of the Korean War did not appear until 1996 when the Korean War Memorial Wall, a 200-foot-long polished granite wall with 516 bronze plaques for each veteran who died in the war, was unveiled at Brampton's Meadowvale Cemetery. The impetus for this memorial, which in its design echoed that of Washington's Vietnam War Memorial, came, it seems, largely from the veterans themselves. To be sure, remembering Canada's involvement in the Second World War took place in a number of locations, particularly at veterans' reunions, Remembrance Day ceremonies, government-sponsored art, the school curriculum, and, more recently, in documentaries and museum exhibits. The latter genres have at times triggered intense debate and conflict, particularly over the role of Allied bombing of Germany during the Second World War. However, the history of the commemoration and collective memory of Canadian participation in the Second World War and Korea awaits its historian.

Historians of commemoration have focused on the collective memory of the "mainstream" memorializing those who might be described as history's "winners." However, the commemoration and collective memory of those whose participation in armed conflict was forgotten, condemned as wrong-headed, even traitorous, or who have straddled both mainstream and alternative modes of commemoration, also has much to teach us. Louis Riel has been, in all likelihood, one of the most controversial and complicated figures in modern Canadian history; his legacy and meaning remain the subject of debate. Hanged in 1885 in Regina, Riel was not commemorated on a national level for almost a century. However, the *Union nationale métisse St-Joseph du Manitoba*, founded a year before his death, built a headstone for Riel's grave at St. Boniface and held ceremonies that depicted Riel as a martyr and hero. In contrast, the provincial and federal governments staged ceremonies and marked historic sites that celebrated Canadian nationalism and British imperialism and memorialized the defeats of Riel, the Metis, and their First Nations allies. By the 1960s, though, with the rise of Aboriginal rights' movements and government-backed initiatives that promoted French-Canadian nationalism, commemorating Riel became more a desirable endeavour for the government and non-Aboriginal Canadians.

During those decades, the Saskatchewan and Manitoba governments commissioned statues of Riel for Regina and Winnipeg, although the Metis and Aboriginal communities saw these representations as controversial and, at times, lacking respect. The government did not consult either community when it commissioned John Nugent to create a statue of Riel in Regina; moreover, it did not invite Aboriginal and Metis people – or even Nugent – to attend the statue's unveiling. Nugent had submitted both modernist and representational designs, the latter of which was chosen by the province: it depicted Riel, standing with his fist clenched as he surrendered at Batoche, as a classical nude wearing a partly open coat that hid only a portion of his body. The statue was contentious from its unveiling until, in 1991, the government moved it from its public site to the city's Mackenzie Art Gallery's vaults. Various groups objected to it for various reasons: the Saskatchewan Family Council did not care for its nudity, while the province's Metis Society wanted a more dignified and respectful statue created by an Aboriginal artist.

In Winnipeg, the newly founded Manitoba Metis Federation lobbied the province in 1967 to have a statue of Riel as part of the province's 1970 centennial celebrations. However, like Nugent's sculpture, Marcien Lemay and Louis Gauthier's abstract figure, unveiled for both the government and Metis community members, sparked debate and sometimes outright hostility. Lemay and Gauthier depicted Riel as being anguished, trapped between two half-cylinders, with his name and the saying (in both French and English) "I know that through the Grace of God, I am the founder of Manitoba" etched at the top of the statue. For some, the statue was a travesty of Riel's legacy and an insult; others were simply unhappy with commemorating Riel at all, seeing him as a traitor who deserved his fate. Over the years, the statue was vandalized, and in the 1980s, Metis activists organized marches and held sit-ins aimed at having it removed; in 1995, the province moved it to the Collège St. Boniface. The Manitoba Metis Federation then commissioned another statue: Miguel Joyal's sculpture of a statesman-like looking Riel, holding a scroll meant to represent the 1870 Manitoba Act, and wearing a suit, moccasins, and Metis sash, won out. Federation members attended the 1996 ceremony, which was marked by the presence of the Metis flag. Yet the public also criticized the statue for being historically incorrect and uninteresting; one commentator wrote in the *Winnipeg Free Press* that it resembled an insurance agent.

Statues, though, were not the only ways in which Riel's memory was revived in the 1960s. Artists and writers had made use of Riel since at least the 1920s, with French writer

Maurice Constantin-Weyer's 1925 fictionalized biography titled *La Bourrasque,* which was translated into English in 1930 as *A Martyr's Folly.* In 1967, Canadian composer Harry Somers and writer Mavor Moore collaborated on a three-act opera, titled simply *Louis Riel*; the opera was first produced by the Canadian Opera Company and supported by the Canadian Centennial Commission, the Canada Council, and the Province of Ontario's Council for the Arts. The opera dealt with the events of both 1869–70 and 1885; critics described it as "vigorous," "brash," "exciting," and "one of the most imaginative and powerful scores to have been written in this century." First performed at Toronto's O'Keefe Centre, *Louis Riel* then played at Montreal's *Place des Arts* and in 1975 was revived in Toronto and toured to Ottawa and the Kennedy Centre (it also was broadcast on CBC-TV in 1969). *Louis Riel* was followed by a CBC-TV film, *Riel,* and, in 2003, by Canadian cartoonist Chester Brown's widely read graphic novel, *Louis Riel: A Comic-Strip Biography.*

At the civic level, Saskatoon celebrated Riel during the 1960s with "Louis Riel Day," a summer event held in the city's downtown that was marked with various athletic events and competitions. Edmonton followed this example in 1985 with celebrations that focused on Riel and then expanded to "Metis week." Furthermore, in 1992, both federal and provincial governments officially recognized Riel as Manitoba's founder. Fifteen years later, when Manitoba's government wished to find a name for its new February holiday, it invited the province's schoolchildren to submit suggestions: Riel's name was the winning entry. Important though these gestures have been, Riel's memory is a complicated one, since as the "father of Manitoba" he is remembered as the leader of the 1869–70 uprising that led to the province's foundation (and, in the eyes of some historians, the dispossession of a number of the Metis from lands promised to them by the Crown) – less so, perhaps, for his role in 1885.

While a number of bills calling for Riel's pardon by the federal government have been unsuccessful, it may be that the Canadian public thinks otherwise. In 2003, CBC-TV staged a simulated retrial of Riel on both its English-language Newsworld channel and Radio Canada's Réseau de l'information, asking its viewers to vote on the final verdict. Of the program's 10,000 viewers, 87 per cent entered a verdict of "not guilty." Riel also appeared on the list of great Canadians for CBC-TV's 2007 program, *The Greatest Canadian,* coming in at number eleven out of 100.

As well as Riel, the Mackenzie-Papineau Battalion, which fought from 1937 to 1939 in Spain as part of the International Brigades, illustrates the political complexities of public memorialization. The "Mac-Paps" fought against the troops of the fascist general Francisco Franco, who led an insurrection against the Republican Popular Front government and was supported by the governments of Italy and Germany. Composed of trade union, Cooperative Commonwealth Federation, and Communist Party members, and named after the leaders of the 1837 Rebellion, over 1,500 Canadians volunteered to fight for democracy (despite the Spanish government's pleas for political support, food, and weapons from Western democracies, only the Soviet Union sent limited assistance). Half of the battalion was either killed or went missing; of those who survived, a number were wounded. The Mac-Paps were welcomed home by their communities and the Canadian people; one of their members, Dr. Norman Bethune, went on to work as an ally in Mao Zedong's Communist army and gained great respect from the Chinese people.

The Canadian government, though, declared Canadian participation in foreign wars illegal and refused to recognize the Mac-Paps' contribution to international democracy. While some members of the brigade fought for Canada in the Second World War, others were barred because of their supposed "political unreliability." As well, the federal government did not grant the Mac-Paps formal recognition in Remembrance Day ceremonies or on its war memorials, nor were the survivors eligible for veterans' benefits. It was not until the 1990s that memorials to the battalion began to appear in Canadian cities' parks, city halls, and legislative buildings, ones put up because of the persistence of the battalions' survivors and their supporters. For example, in 2001, a monument honouring the battalion was unveiled in Ottawa, on Green Island in the Rideau River. Designed by Sudbury's Oryst Sawchuk, an architect and artist, the plaque on the monument lists all 1,546 Canadians who went to Spain. It also provides an excerpt from the speech given by Dolores Ibárruri, *La Pasionaria*, to the International Brigades upon their disbanding in 1938. Her speech honours their heroism, promises the love and gratitude of the Spanish people, and – most tellingly for our purposes – vows that their examples of democracy, solidarity, and universality will not be forgotten.

The Mackenzie-Papineau Battalion was not the only group of Canadians whose overseas participation under "foreign" command fell outside of the Canadian government's aegis and, therefore, official commemorations. Those 30,000 Canadians (which included fifty Mohawks from Kahnawake, near Montreal) who volunteered to fight in the Vietnam War for the American government have been publicly remembered largely through the efforts of Vietnam veterans. The first such monument was erected in Melocheville, Quebec (a small city south of Montreal), and was put up in 1990 by the Association Québécoise des Vétérans du Vietnam; it was dedicated to those who died or went missing in action between 1964 and 1975. Five years later in Windsor, Ontario, a group of Vietnam veterans erected a privately funded monument of black granite known as the "North Wall." The group placed the monument in the city's Assumption Park close to the Detroit River; the "North Wall" lists the names of 103 Canadians who died in Southeast Asia. Perhaps it is not surprising that both monuments have been erected in cities close to the Canada-U.S. border; Windsor, for example, has been long known for its cross-border connections to the United States. The contested memory of the Vietnam War also has entered Canadian discourses around commemoration in debates over Vietnam War resisters, many of whom entered Canada in the 1960s and 1970s and became part of Canadian society. In 2004, in the town of Nelson, British Columbia, local activists and former resisters' attempts to honour their community with a reunion and the unveiling of a statue, *Welcoming Peace*, drew the attention – and opposition – of conservative media from the United States, with the result that the town refused to allow the statue to be built. Instead, the town offered to sanction a more generic monument that celebrated Canada as a general haven for refugees, a substitution that the organizers perceived as muting the more pointed and political message of *Welcoming Peace* and which they rejected. The Doukhobor Village Museum in nearby Castlegar initially offered to display the statue but decided against it, with the result that the statue is housed privately in Nelson.

Canadian history has been marked by other kinds of conflicts, such as struggles between labour, capital, and the Canadian state, that at times have resulted in violence. To be sure, commemorations of strikes and other forms of workers' public activism have not tended to receive the same amount of official attention or financial support as have Canadians' engagements in overseas wars. However, Canadians have memorialized twentieth-century events such as the 1919 Winnipeg General Strike or the Estevan, Saskatchewan, coal strike and riot of 1931 in a number of ways. In the 1980s, Toronto artist Robert Kell completed his series of paintings, entitled "Winnipeg 1919" and begun in the 1970s, that commemorated the strike; his exhibit was timed to open with Winnipeg's Labour Day Festival. More recently, the strike has been the subject of various museum exhibits, a walking tour of downtown Winnipeg, and in 2010, *Strike! The Musical*, by playwright Danny Schur. In the case of Estevan, three miners, Peter Markunas, Julian Gryshko, and Nick Nargan, were shot by the RCMP during a miners' parade, an event remembered in the town itself, albeit with some degree of contestation. The strikers were buried in a common grave, its stone marked by a red star and the inscription "Murdered by the RCMP," an epitaph that has alternately been erased and restored. As well as the miners' grave, on 29 September 1981, the provincial labour movement and the Estevan Labour Coordinating Committee erected a plaque, named "Coal Miner's Corner," at the town's courthouse. Now the site of annual 28 April "Day of Mourning" ceremonies for workers who have died on the job, the plaque memorializes both the miners who died on "Black Tuesday," 29 September, and all those who contributed to the area's labour movement. Moreover, in 1997, the Saskatchewan Federation of Labour set up another plaque to memorialize the miners, one unveiled by Peter Markunas's widow.

Commemorations of Canadians' military participation, whether overseas or at home, illuminate a number of important themes and raise thought-provoking questions. Although historians have long been sceptical of the claim that Canada has been a "peaceable kingdom," as its citizens' involvement in war was either minimal and reluctant or having occurred strictly because of the imperial tie, such a claim often resonates with the general public. It is often argued, for example, that Canadians' participation in the Afghanistan War and civilian support for the country's troops – exemplified by the renaming of an eastern stretch of Highway 401 in Ontario as the "Highway of Heroes" – represents a new stage in the formation of national identity. Yet examining the way in which war has been remembered in Canada suggests a somewhat different history. Even if Canada's participation in, for example, the South African War or the First World War was controversial or induced by external forces, the alacrity with which these, and other conflicts, were remembered suggests that a considerable

number of Canadians strongly believed in the need to commemorate soldiers and battles. Furthermore, while not
wishing to deny or obscure the history of opposition to
these conflicts – whether on the part of French-Canadian
nationalists, the left, or pacifists – the eagerness with which
many Canadians acted on a voluntary basis to erect monuments, plant trees, purchase souvenirs, and turn out for
Remembrance Day services suggests that these acts of commemoration were not directed by the state; in fact, the state
often lagged behind local committees in the work of commemoration. To be sure, many of these committees and
individuals were either middle or upper-middle class. Yet it
is striking how members of groups – Aboriginals, African-
Canadians, Japanese-Canadians, workers – whose wartime
contributions were rarely recognized by the mainstream
sought to make their histories visible and demanded official
recognition of their sacrifices from the Canadian government and, by extension, the Canadian public. For members
of these communities, the legacy of military participation
was an important aspect of their histories, not least because
it played a crucial role in claiming the rights of a Canadian
citizen.

5

Commemoration, Historical Preservation, and the Canadian State

Governments – federal, provincial, and municipal – have played a variety of roles in historical preservation, restoration, and commemorative practices. In nineteenth-century France, for example, the state clearly was instrumental in founding and managing institutions such as museums or historic sites and in shaping (or at least attempting to shape) the contours of national memories and histories. Other nations, such as Britain, the United States, and Australia, saw government "intervention" in this area develop more slowly and unevenly over time. From the late nineteenth century, governments in a number of countries began to assume more responsibility for funding and managing institutions, as well as providing the legislative framework to take over and preserve historic sites. However, private individuals, associations, and – not least – private capital also continued to have a significant presence in creating "public" histories.

In many ways Canada's trajectory was little different. The various nineteenth- and early-twentieth-century initiatives and projects discussed in the previous chapters – monuments, pageants, historical societies, written texts, and commemorations of the First World War – frequently were undertaken on a voluntary basis or, if government-sponsored, occurred because influential and persistent individuals pushed levels of government to act. However, rather than assume that this meant simply government indifference to the nation's history and its citizens' collective memory, we should take into account the Canadian state's role in cultural policy more broadly, the fact that competing views of government's position vis-à-vis historic sites existed, and the fact that the Dominion government may well have lacked the funds necessary to embark on ambitious preservation and restoration programs, as well as the means of raising such monies. Furthermore, although it has received less attention from historians, the history of Canadian museums suggests similar complicated relationships to the state and the public domain.

Marking historic sites, though, was not the first sign of the Canadian government's interest in preserving the past. In 1871, Henry H. Miles, a member of the Quebec Literary Historical Society, forwarded a petition to the governor general and the House of Commons that called for the creation of a public archival repository. Signed by fifty-seven elite English- and French-speaking residents of Quebec City, Montreal, and Ottawa, the petition reflected growing frustration with the state of written records that dealt with Canada's history: they were spread out in sites across the country and abroad, were not catalogued, and were vulnerable to damage and neglect. Miles's petition resulted in the appointment of journalist Douglas Brymner as "Senior Second Class Clerk" by the Minister of Agriculture. His was not, though, the first such appointment in Canada, since in 1857 Thomas B. Akins was made the commissioner of Nova Scotia's public records. Well-connected and with a keen interest in Canada's history, Brymner travelled across the country and discovered that many important records were held by individuals or families (he also supported Akins in his endeavours to keep British military records that pertained to Canada from leaving the country). Brymner also crossed the Atlantic to visit London's War Office, Public Record Office, Tower of London, British Museum, and Hudson's Bay Company holdings. While he was away, the abbé Hospice-Anthelme Verreau, under the direction of the Minister of Agriculture, Joseph H. Pope, visited France to look at documents from the period of French imperial control before 1759. Although Brymner hoped to undertake a large-scale project of transcription of the records, the economic crisis of the 1870s put his plans on hold until the end of the decade. As well, the government created two competing bodies to deal with the country's documented past. In 1873, the Secretary of State appointed a "Keeper of the Records," the biographer Henry J. Morgan, whose mandate was to look after the records of federal departments (it would not be until the 1950s and 1960s that the Archives would take over responsibility for federal government records). With the help of staff hired in the late 1870s, Brymner carried on with his transcribing, his focus the conquest of New France and the American Revolution. In 1888, the American Historical Association praised his work, and by the 1890s, historians began to use the thousands of archival volumes created by his department. By the time he died in 1902, his unofficial title was that of "Dominion Archivist" and the Archives held over 3,000 volumes; the majority of these were transcriptions of original documents produced by the British and French colonial administrations.

Brymner's successor, Quebec legislative librarian Arthur Doughty, both intensified and expanded his predecessor's work. Doughty had been influenced by the "scientific" study of history that dominated academic departments in the United States and Europe and believed that the Dominion Archivist should promote archival research as a way of promoting and strengthening Canadian history. Doughty believed that government needed to take a more active part in supporting Canadians' interest in their history. One of Doughty's more notable and publicly visible contributions was the expansion of the Archives' holdings. Not only did the transcription program continue to grow, it was complemented by acquisitions of other media, so that textual materials, photographs, and map were joined by engravings, paintings, watercolours, and topographical surveys.

Over the 1900s, the Archives' budget grew (from $11,000 in 1903 to $50,000 in 1907) and it acquired its own building. In 1912, Parliament passed the Public Archives Act, which gave it the status of a department and moved it from the Department of Agriculture to the supervision of the Secretary of State, where it would remain until 1987. With fellow historian Adam Shortt, Doughty published a number of guides and catalogues, as well as the twenty-three-volume *Canada and Its Provinces*, the latter intended to promote Canadian nationalism through the country's history. The National Archives spread its influence across the country by the establishment of offices in cities in Quebec and the Maritimes and by the work of its agents in Ontario and the Prairie provinces. Doughty established relationships with provincial archives, universities, and historians. By the 1920s, he expanded the Archives' work in Europe. As well, during that decade, the Archives ran a summer school for graduate students, was involved in the founding of the Canadian Historical Association and the *Canadian Historical Review*, and created kits for schoolchildren that teachers could use to teach history. When he retired in 1935, Doughty was made a knight of the Order of the British Empire and, after his death in 1936, was honoured by the creation of a statue in his memory, the only one erected to a federal public servant.

While Brymner and Doughty were involved in gathering and preserving the textual records of the past, a number of their contemporaries were concerned with the need for the classification, cataloguing, and preservation of historic sites and landmarks. By the late 1880s, members of historical societies and patriotic groups, such as the Société St-Jean-Baptiste-de-Québec, as well as more broadly based cultural groups, started to form national, regional, and local associations aimed at promoting Canadian nationalism through shared notions of Canadian history and significant historical sites. To be sure, they differed in the particular historical markers they chose and the reasons behind their choices varied. Ideological motives prompted some to argue for the significance of the Niagara-area War of 1812 battlefields of Lundy's Lane and Stoney Creek. Others were worried about the threat of deterioration of other sites, as in the City of Hamilton's decision to buy Dundurn Castle, the home of Allan McNab, the Upper Canadian Conservative lawyer, land speculator, railway promoter, and politician. Still others were concerned about sites that held archaeological and scientific interest, such as Ontario archaeologist David Boyle's passion for Indigenous sites in southern Ontario.

In the Maritimes, notions of Britain's centrality to the region's history or, for some, Acadian nationalism, played an influential role. Less overtly educational preservation took place, unlike, for example, that at Lundy's Lane. To be sure, the Nova Scotia Historical Society, the provincial archives, and the curator of the province's museum were concerned with the preservation of historic buildings, while in New Brunswick the "loyalist legacy" was a significant narrative for those involved in public history. However, the restoration of Annapolis Royal, which by the late nineteenth century was controlled by the Department of Militia and Defense, demonstrates that no one "national" narrative necessarily prevailed in the Maritimes; a visitor to Annapolis Royal would be greeted with multiple interpretations of the site's history. It was seen as a place of early European settlement in North American (Habitation Port Royal), the former centre of Acadie (Port Royal), and then the gathering place for American Loyalists (Fort Anne). These interpretations of Annapolis Royal were very different from the more homogenous nationalist narratives that captured the imaginations of historical preservationists in Ontario.

The ruined fortress of Louisbourg also presented its own particular challenges. Built by the French in the eighteenth century as a central part of its Atlantic defence, then captured by the British in 1745, and destroyed and rebuilt in 1758, Louisbourg in many ways exemplifies the complicated relationships between levels of government and the private sector in Canadian historical preservation. Although known today as a major "national" site, in the early twentieth century the site was not even publicly owned. In 1903, a retired naval captain, D.J. Kennelly, bought it and attempted to establish it as a tourist attraction. Kennelly attempted to fix the fortress by propping up the surviving brickwork with timber and patching the mortar; he also built a restaurant in its ruins. Moreover, in an attempt to get more sustained and widespread support for restoration, he formed the Louisbourg Memorial Association and canvassed those British regiments who'd been at the fort's second siege to support his work. Kennelly also lobbied the Dominion government for funds and received $5,000 for his efforts. By 1906, Kennelly convinced the provincial government of the need for legislation that treated the fort and its surrounding burial ground as a historic monument of the Dominion.

However, to attract more members of the public who were willing to pay his entrance fee of twenty-five cents, Kennelly needed better public access, since Louisbourg was difficult to reach by land. His attempts to have a rail and ferry link that would stretch from Ontario (presumably to attract tourists from that province) to the site were unsuccessful and Kennelly managed only to get a railway right of way granted. On his death in 1912, Kennelly left a number of legal questions surrounding the fort's ownership; it was not until after the First World War that the Dominion government started to assume responsibility for Louisbourg. Furthermore, although Kennelly saw the fort as part of British imperial history, another perspective on Louisbourg started to develop; scholars such as John George Bourinot were beginning to claim it for the French-Canadian past.

By the early twentieth century, a number of individuals began to call for a more national and centralized approach to historic sites. The Committee for the Preservation of Scenic and Historic Places in Canada was formed in 1901, its membership composed of prominent intellectuals, journalists, and political figures such as Benjamin Sulte,

James LeMoine, John Willison, George Denison, and John George Bourinot. Many of these men were members of the Royal Society of Canada, an organization formed in 1882 by the governor general to promote scholarly work in the sciences and humanities and bring together like-minded institutions and individuals. The Committee also had been inspired by Britain's National Trust, an organization founded in 1895 by Victorian philanthropists who believed the country's coastline, countryside, and buildings were endangered by industrial and urban growth. By 1907, the Committee decided that a national body was needed to deal with the volume and scope of work across Canada and renamed itself, first, the Historic Landmarks Association and, then, the National Battlefields Commission. Restoring the Plains of Abraham became its first priority and many of its members were involved in the Champlain Tercentenary. As the Commission lacked the means to tackle specific restoration projects, it instead used local historical societies, who lobbied the Dominion government to recognize particular certain monuments, buildings, ruins, battlefields, and forts as being of national historic significance. Quite likely the Commission wanted the government to pass legislation to prevent the destruction of historic sites; however, it saw its function as that of an advisory board which would screen local applications and advise the government on their importance.

After the war, the Dominion government decided that it would prefer to set up its own organizations, the Historic Sites and Monuments Board (HSMBC or the Board) and Parks Canada, to deal with historic sites and the Canadian landscape (the Historic Landmarks Association became part of the Canadian Historical Association). The HSMBC consisted of volunteers from various historical communities and organizations, their role that of an advisory board which was to make recommendations that certain landscapes and buildings be recognized as having historical significance. The Parks branch shifted quite a bit over the course of the twentieth century and made its home in a number of departments; overall, though, its mandate was to work on the physical preservation of certain "natural" landscapes, creating them as parks, and to oversee certain sites, Louisbourg being one of them.

One of the central questions that dominated these organizations' work was a tension or disagreement over commemoration – putting up plaques that would educate the public about a building's or site's historical significance – and preservation of places threatened with destruction or decay. While the HSMBC changed its direction over the course of the twentieth century, a change that was particularly noticeable by the 1960s, the decisions that were made and implemented in the 1920s and 1930s had important consequences for public history that, to some extent, are still felt today.

Although the Board's members included representatives from across Canada, it is not an exaggeration to say that the perspectives of those from Ontario and Quebec dominated. In the 1920s and 1930s, two of the most prominent and influential members were from Ontario: Brigadier-General Ernest Cruikshank and James Coyne. Originally a member of the militia and a gentleman farmer in Welland, Cruikshank's central interest in Canadian history was the War of 1812. Cruikshank was linked to the federal government's bureaucracy in a number of ways, as he was the director of the Military Historical Section at the Department of Militia and Defence, a position he held until 1921. In 1906, Cruikshank was elected to the Royal Society and served as the Ontario Historical Society's president from 1920 to 1922; through this work he had built a reputation as a solid and thorough historian. While Cruikshank believed that historians must immerse themselves in primary sources, strive for "scientific" objectivity, and avoid nationalist biases, he nevertheless also saw Canada's past as full of moral lessons in nationalism and loyalty, a belief which shaped his approach to public commemoration. In Cruikshank's opinion, for instance, the patriotic behaviour of the War of 1812's militia, not William Lyon Mackenzie's leadership of the 1837 Rebellion, should be commemorated. Despite numerous requests from the York Pioneer and Historical Society in Toronto, the Board repeatedly refused to grant formal recognition to the city's first mayor (until the 1930s, the sole site associated with Mackenzie and his supporters was Montgomery's Tavern on Toronto's Yonge Street). Cruikshank also believed historical narratives were best conveyed through documentary and textual sources; history, in his eyes, was meant to instruct, not to appeal to the emotions or sensations through visual media such as material culture (Cruikshank also argued that local museums should not be funded by the state).

Cruikshank's counterpart, James Coyne, was a lawyer by training and had worked as the County Registrar in the southwestern Ontario city of St. Thomas. Like Cruikshank, Coyne had been a member of the militia and as a teenager had served against the Fenians; he also had been president of the OHS. However, unlike Cruikshank, Coyne was particularly interested in the pre-contact history of Ontario, as well as its early exploration and settlement. He argued for the preservation of Ojibwa historical narratives and for documentation of the geographic expansion of the French into the province, calling for the marking of places such as Port Dover, Midland, Sault Ste. Marie, and Port Arthur.

Although not quite as dominant a member as Cruikshank and Coyne (partly because he died in 1923, not long after the HSMBC's establishment), Benjamin Sulte also played a pivotal role in determining the Board's direction. Originally from Trois-Rivières, Sulte had served in the militia, as well as working as a journalist, translator, and civil servant. While he drew the wrath of some of his fellow historians in Quebec because of his scepticism over the Church's role in New France, Sulte had a romantic affinity with an epic and heroic version of New France's history. Sulte was eager to see his home town nominated for a number of notable dates and achievements: as the birthplace of an important explorer, Pierre Gaultier de Varennes, sieur de La Vérendrye; as the site of an important "Canadian" victory over American invaders, the Battle of Trois-Rivières; and as the location of one of Canada's earliest industries, the St. Maurice Forges.

Under Cruikshank, Coyne, and Sulte, then, certain places, events, and individuals helped shape narratives of Canada's history: particular types of Aboriginal settlement, French explorers in Western Canada, heroic defenders of the colony before the conquest, the Loyalists, and the War of 1812. These narratives were promoted through commemorative plaques fixed on or near buildings and landscapes, not their large-scale restoration or preservation. To some extent, the Board was hampered by a lack of funding. However, its leading members were not interested in lobbying for such funds. Although regional promoters of "heritage" and tourism argued for the restoration or preservation of buildings and sites as a way of attracting tourists and generating jobs, such considerations were not priorities for Cruikshank, Coyne, and Sulte. Instead, they saw themselves as an elite whose superior education made them responsible for the tutelage and instruction of Canadians, particularly youth and new immigrants.

To be sure, the Board was not insensible to the need for some preservation work. It recommended that a number of forts both in the Maritimes, including Louisbourg, and in Western Canada should be preserved. However, the problem with these recommendations was their lack of detail. Moreover, the Parks branch, charged with undertaking such work, lacked the necessary experts who could advise on the historical materials and techniques needed for such projects. They often were forced to call in and rely on local entrepreneurs whose interests in historical preservation might differ from those of the HSMBC or Parks branch, as they saw the sites less for their didactic potential in teaching nationalism and more as a way of boosting local economies.

Although the Parks branch took over northwest Saskatchewan's Fort Pelly, as they believed it to be an important site in the history of the Northwest and the Hudson's Bay Company, the Parks branch turned down the chance to acquire Lower Fort Garry when it found the Bay had leased it to a local automobile club. Indeed, public dissatisfaction grew with the apparent slowness of the Parks branch to acquire properties. Maritimers were irritated by the state of Louisbourg, Ontario Members of Parliament asked questions in the House of Commons about the lack of preservation in Ontario, and Westerners wrote angry letters to the Board claiming that it was neglecting their region.

Furthermore, not all those involved with the Parks branch were interested only in historical sites; some believed that landscape was equally important. James Harkin, a prominent civil servant appointed commissioner of the branch in 1911, wanted to set up national parks in Western Canada, especially in the Rocky Mountains, that would celebrate the country's natural landscape and would bring visitors to the region. However, to do so Harkin needed funding for the expansion and improvement of roads, since tourism in the 1920s was increasingly becoming tied to automobiles. Moreover, the Parks branch lacked legislation that would give it authority to acquire properties. Harkin spearheaded such a proposal in 1920, one which would have given the branch sweeping powers to acquire historic property and grant temporary preservation orders so that properties facing destruction could be seized. It did not make it to the House of Commons, though, as the federal government balked at putting aside the funds that the legislation would have entailed. Despite Harkin's pressure on the HSMBC to widen its vision of commemoration to include more social and economic history, a lack of government policy held back work on preservation and restoration.

Thus the Parks branch was forced to do its work on an ad hoc, informal basis, subjecting it to pressure exerted by local organizations and the dynamics of locality and region. For example, the Maritimes acquired more sites, since there was a greater push in that area to acquire properties and preserve them. Since forts were already owned by the federal government, it was relatively easier for the Parks branch to take them over; prior ownership partly accounts for their predominance in the branch's holdings. The Board's interests also continued to be dominated by military history, since Cruikshank continued to serve as its chair and Sulte's death meant that representation from Quebec was inconsistent; few Quebec historians wished to expose themselves to the prejudices and condescension of their anglophone colleagues. In 1924, the Board passed a resolution that deliberately excluded graveyards and churches from its mandate. Certain sites also posed particular challenges for "national" historic interpretations; the Northwest Rebellion, for example, was perceived in different ways by different groups in Quebec, Ontario, and the Western provinces.

Despite the dominance of particular perspectives, though, the decade was not marked by complete consensus about the HSMBC or Parks branch's work. To be sure, the latter resumed work on Louisbourg in 1920, a development sparked by examples south of the border, such as Fort Ticonderoga on Lake Champlain and, in particular, the reconstruction of Virginia's colonial Williamsburg. Historic sites, it seemed, could become successful tourist attractions once fixed up as living museums and not left as ruins. The Board itself also saw an improvement in representation from the Western provinces and British Columbia, although that did not lead to an automatic increase in the number of sites commemorated in both those areas. While Alberta groups wished to preserve Aboriginal buffalo pounds, the Board held back, not wishing to be associated with the destruction of the prairie buffalo. They also refused to designate Fort Whoop-Up a national historic site, believing its association with the American whisky trade disqualified it. Commemorative plaques that the Board put up at Batoche and Cut Knife Hill, both significant sites in the Northwest Rebellion, ended up offending Quebec and the Metis, as it initially refused to put up bilingual plaques. As well, the first version of the Cut Knife Hill plaque's text did not make it clear that the Canadian militia had been defeated in its raid on Poundmaker's camp and referred to Aboriginal people as "rebels." Thus the HSMBC affronted members of Saskatchewan's Poundmaker Reserve, who had surrendered land for the cairn on which the plaque had been placed.

Moreover, commemorations of Acadian history at Grand-Pré in the 1920s, which the Board approached in a spirit of biculturalism as a means of mending the rift between French and English Canada, ran into opposing narratives of the 1755 *Grand Dérangement* or Expulsion. The Board wished to commemorate first the "Battle of Grand-Pré," a military clash in 1747 between Canadian-Acadian-Aboriginal forces and a New England militia garrison, which resulted in the death of the latter's commander, Colonel Arthur Noble; the Expulsion came a distinct second on their list of priorities. The resulting controversy was fuelled by the stance taken by local English-Canadians, who saw Noble's death as a "massacre" and downplayed the injustices and suffering endured by the deported Acadians. Imperialist attitudes towards francophones – not to mention Aboriginals, Metis, and recent immigrants – helped shape the Board's decisions.

While the early 1930s did not produce dramatic shifts in the government's attitude towards public history, the Board and the Parks branch showed some signs of change. The arrival of Nova Scotia's provincial archivist D.C. Harvey, for example, brought a stronger voice for regional history to the Board's deliberations. Coyne's replacement, historian Fred Landon, believed in an Ontario history more ethnically and racially heterogeneous and linked to the United States in a positive way; in particular, Landon's work focused on the history of Ontario's African-Canadian communities. Landon also saw the Rebellion of 1837 as a progressive event that led to the establishment of responsible government. However, the question of legislation that would protect buildings threatened by neglect or direct destruction remained complicated. Across the country, responses to this problem varied considerably. In Quebec, architectural groups and other associations called for greater protection of the province's "traditional" architecture, seeing it as part of its collective heritage. While an inventory of such buildings in Quebec existed, there was no accompanying legislation to protect them. In Ontario, while groups such as the Architectural Conservancy of Ontario, founded in 1933, tried to preserve Loyalist houses, especially in Niagara-on-the-Lake, no protective legislation was enacted until after the Second World War. British Columbia was the only other province to pass such laws; in its case, they were aimed at protecting Indigenous peoples' artefacts. However, a lack of money to enforce the legislation meant that they were not very effective.

The most significant change in the Canadian government's policy came about because of a national calamity, the Great Depression. As part of its attempt to generate employment, Prime Minister William Lyon Mackenzie King's government allocated greater amounts of funds to the Parks branch: in its 1938 budget, it received $2 million, of which $99,000 were allocated to historic sites. These funds were followed by a further $65,000 the following year. Not surprisingly, the Parks branch rushed to complete work on Louisbourg and on other forts, as well as starting new developments at Annapolis Royal, Wilfrid Laurier's House in Saint-Lin, and Fort Malden in southern Ontario. It also dispensed large amounts of money for work at Halifax's Citadel and to Quebec City for its historic walls. Yet despite the intensification of this work, the HSMBC was ambivalent about historic reconstruction, primarily because certain of its members held philosophical concerns about its ahistorical nature. Would putting in roads, museums, and interpretive centres, not to mention safety features such as fences and barricades, destroy a site's historic integrity, even though such work was seen as necessary if the public were to enjoy it in a safe and accessible manner? Historic preservationists often wanted to maintain a site in its original state, while protecting it from encroachments and further natural deterioration. However, by the 1930s, aesthete and critic John Ruskin's belief that any restoration was destructive, a view that had been very influential in the nineteenth century, was beginning to be eclipsed by those who saw Williamsburg as setting a leading (and potentially lucrative) example.

Although these tensions were not solved (and, indeed, in some circles still remain), in the late 1930s, the HSMBC began to look at a wider range of sites. In Ontario, it took over lighthouses, oil wells, cheese factories, and recognized Aboriginal treaties as historically significant; on the Prairies, the founding of the provinces, Aboriginal leaders, and the saving of the prairie buffalo fell under its aegis. But not all sites were deemed to be of equal historical interest. Parochialism and racial prejudice resulted in the exclusion of some Canadians from its commemorative activities. When Jacob Livinson, chair of the citizenship committee of Montreal's City Improvement League suggested in 1945 that the Commission recognize the first synagogue in Canada, his request was rejected. In responding to Livinson, Commission board member Edouard-Fabre Surveyer wrote that he "was not particularly interested in the commemoration of Jewish activities." Surveyer also rejected a fellow Board member's suggestion that the Commission erect a monument to the presence of 400 African-Canadians who lived on Vancouver Island before 1858, writing that he did not see that the "immigration of Negroes is a fact to rejoice upon." Another member, Father Antoine D'Eschambault, similarly perceived Mennonite immigration as an unsuitable subject for memorialization; the Board also rejected a request to designate the first Ukrainian settlement in Canada.

While the Second World War's outbreak meant that the Board's activities were put on hold, postwar reconstruction and, in particular, the influence of the Massey Commission on Arts and Letters (1949–51) brought matters of culture and history to the forefront of policy discussions. Although the Commission called for greater government involvement in cultural funding and policy development, it was loath to call for more direct intervention around historic sites. The commissioners knew that a range of opinions existed across Canada about the definitions of "national" historic sites. As well, many of those who submitted briefs wished for more preservation of domestic architecture, which did not interest the commissioners. Vincent Massey and historian Hilda Neatby, the latter one of the most prominent and better-known commissioners, were interested in commemoration – erecting plaques that would educate the public about the historical significance of particular sites – even though the local groups that spoke to them were concerned with preserving buildings and landscapes. Moreover, despite the expansion of its work in the late 1930s, the Board's attitude towards determining sites of historic significance did not shift dramatically. When asked to present a list of criteria for sites of national interest, its submission emphasized discovery, exploration, French and English settlement, and the Loyalist defence of Upper Canada.

Yet changes in the federal government's attitude towards culture and Canadian history specifically were underway in the 1950s: the National Library, Public Archives of Canada, and National Museum expanded; new agencies, such as CBC-TV and the National Film Board, were created; and a great more attention began to be paid to the historic sites program than had previously been the case. In 1953, the government passed the Historic Sites and Monuments Act, which gave the program a legislative framework and base. Under the terms of the act, each province would be represented by an appointed Board member, with an extra member appointed from Ontario and Quebec; it also would have representation from the archival community. The Board could designate buildings as historic sites based on their architectural significance, a provision for which preservationists from the Maritimes had been lobbying since the 1930s.

While the HSMBC thus saw its mandate expand, at the provincial level heritage agencies and provincially run historic sites became more prolific. The provincial government in Ontario, for example, became increasingly involved in large-scale projects. The expansion of the St. Lawrence Seaway threatened a number of buildings deemed to be of historic interest (as well as demolishing entire communities); the St. Lawrence Development Commission then moved them, restored them, and furnished them with period items. The result was Upper Canada Village near Morrisburg, in eastern Ontario, which, staffed with costumed interpreters (much like Louisbourg), was influenced by the open-air folk museums of late-nineteenth-century Sweden and Henry Ford's museum at Greenfield, Michigan.

Sainte-Marie-among-the-Hurons in southern Ontario's Midland, the site of a seventeenth-century French Catholic mission, was yet another example of the province's interest in historical reconstruction. From the early twentieth century, Midland had been claimed by the Jesuit Order as a historically important religious site and anthropologists started to excavate it the 1940s. The efforts (not to mention political connections) of local businessman Bill Cranston in the 1950s and early 1960s helped draw the province into the reconstruction of Midland. The province saw the site as a potential tourist attraction, an example of a French and Catholic settlement at a time when biculturalism and bilingualism were seen as more desirable, and an example of early provincial technological innovation through its "locked waterway" (no matter that the latter was not a historically accurate description of the site's ditches). However, in its desire to make Midland serve a number of mid-twentieth-century needs, those involved in its rebuilding and promotion focused only on the Jesuits and ignored the historical presence of the Wendat First Nations. Such a decision surprised a number of visitors who had expected a much more prominent First Nations presence at the site. The concept of designated heritage monuments, introduced in Quebec in 1956, brought a new dimension to the state's role. Based on French legislation, these monuments were privately owned buildings which were recognized by the province and then protected from destruction or significant alterations by heritage building codes. Quebec then set up its own Ministry of Culture in 1961; other provinces followed suit in the 1960s and 1970s. These ministries tended to combine the arts, historic sites, archives, and museums with tourism and recreation, a perception of the relation between the two areas that became increasingly common. In this, as in other aspects of provincial agencies' practices, little differentiated the general approach of the provinces, which often followed the federal model. After the initial phase of recognition and commemoration, historic sites were often set up as recreational and tourist developments. Although originally perceived as the "junior" counterpart of their federal siblings, as provincial identities became more visibly robust over the course of the 1960s, provincial organizations began to argue for greater jurisdiction over sites and, in some cases, saw themselves as rivals to the federal government.

Historic preservationists were faced with new challenges in the postwar period, ones that government could only partly address. As postwar urban redevelopment brought new or expanded highways and commercial buildings in downtown cores, nineteenth- and early-twentieth-century homes and other buildings, seen as representing stagnation and halting "progress," were vulnerable and threatened with destruction. Indeed, a number of Canadian towns and cities lost such buildings to wreckers' balls. In the face of these losses, a number of existing local groups either mobilized or were organized to lobby against such practices, such as the Architectural Conservancy in Ontario, founded in 1933, and the Preservation Committee of the Royal Architectural

Institute of Ontario, formed in 1959 and chaired by Eric Arthur, a New-Zealand born, British-trained professor of architecture at the University of Toronto. Yet technical and jurisdictional problems hampered these bodies' activities. While a national inventory of national historic sites with architectural merit existed, preservation of property could only be achieved by its designation as a national historic park, a route that was cumbersome, expensive, and impractical for homes and other buildings in urban settings. Although designating the latter as national historic sites had moral weight, it offered little in the way of practical protection, since provinces, not the federal government, had jurisdiction over private property. Furthermore, by the 1970s, Quebec, Alberta, and Ontario had established their own architectural preservation programs and were not always willing to work cooperatively with the federal government to receive funding. A solution was proposed in the form of Heritage Canada, an independent not-for-profit foundation that would operate at arm's-length from the federal government. Created in 1973 at the suggestion of Jean Chrétien, then prime minister Pierre Trudeau's minister of Indian and Northern Affairs, Heritage Canada was intended to solve the problem of the federal government taking over private property. However, over the long term, Heritage Canada was not adequately funded and thus lacked the resources to acquire buildings. Simultaneously, the federal government began to set up regional offices for Parks Canada in Calgary, Winnipeg, Halifax, Quebec City, and Cornwall to work on historic sites. These offices helped invigorate regional and community heritage preservation, since their staff provided scholarship, planning expertise, and leadership in community efforts to preserve urban heritage.

As much as the work of the HSMBC, Parks Canada, and the various provincial heritage bodies was marked by differences over commemoration versus preservation and restoration or jurisdictional disputes, it was also shaped by notions of the historical significance of certain individuals, events, and processes. Such notions led to others being seen, explicitly or implicitly, as being historically insignificant. One such group whose absence was notable from plaques or sites was Canadian women. From 1919 until 2008, Canadian women comprised only 6 per cent of those commemorated by the HSMBC: 125 designations out of 1,942. Twenty-six of these were sites, sixty-six were persons, and thirty-three were events. In 1923, the Board recognized its first woman, Madeleine de Verchères; in 1927, it placed a plaque at the site of an existing monument to her memory. The plaque asked Canadians to remember the fourteen-year-old Verchères's defence of her family's seigneury against the Iroquois, assisted only by her two young brothers, an elderly servant, and two soldiers. In the 1930s, the Board, thanks to its program of secondary plaques that recognized prominent individuals, honoured the Canadian soprano Emma Albani and Louise McKinney, one of the leaders of the Persons Case, which resulted in Canadian women gaining the right to be appointed to the Senate. Other "women worthies" that the HSMBC designated have been sports figures, such as the women's basketball team the Edmonton Grads and marathon swimmer Marilyn Bell, women nurses in Newfoundland and Quebec, women's religious orders, both Protestant and Catholic, social reformers (the Women's Christian Temperance Union and the Fédération nationale Saint-Jean Baptiste), and certain first-wave feminists, such as Nellie McClung. The Board also recognized figures from the world of literature and the visual arts, most notably painter Emily Carr and writer Lucy Maud Montgomery, although they were more ambivalent about the Mohawk-English poet and performer E. Pauline Johnson. While Johnson was designated a person of historic significance in 1945, for reasons that are not entirely clear she was de-designated in 1961. In 1983, Johnson was restored to her previous status, most likely because of a resurgence of community and academic interest in her life and work.

Other women also did not fare well; female politicians, for example, received far less attention and respect than did their male counterparts. Agnes Macphail, the first woman to be elected to the House of Commons, was placed on the Board's list of distinguished Canadians in 1955 but was removed in 1973. In 1976, the Board decided that Macphail's home in Ceylon, Ontario, was not of national historic or architectural significance; one year later, it declared that Macphail was not historically significant, a decision it reversed in 1985. However, lettering for Macphail's plaque was not completed and approved until 1990; at the time of writing it still has not been put up. It may be that Macphail's leftist and progressive politics – her association with the United Farmers of Ontario, the Progressive Party, and the Cooperative Commonwealth Federation – the fact that she was not clearly identified with the suffrage movement, and her opposition to the government on issues such as prison reform led to her marginalization at the federal level. Her case demonstrates the conservatism and caution of the HSMBC specifically, and of formal, national, commemorative practices, since from the 1960s on, particularly in the Grey-Bruce and Toronto areas, others have recognized Macphail in a number of ways. A Canadian Heritage Minute, schools, parks, awards, a public-speaking contest, a day (the anniversary of her election), and a cairn and a bust in Hopeville, Ontario, have been dedicated to her; many of these tributes either have been linked to causes that promote social justice and equality, or represent Macphail as someone who fought for them.

Another group of female political activists, the "Famous Five," also received mixed treatment from the Board. While Louise McKinney, Nellie McClung, Emily Murphy, Irene Parlby, and Henrietta Muir Edwards were journalists, social reformers, legislators, and suffragists in their own right, they also have been remembered as the group of women who spearheaded the Persons Case. From the late 1930s until the 1960s, HMSBC and Parks Canada recognized each individual woman with plaques that memorialized both their achievements in other areas and their work on the Persons Case. However, citing the presence of these monuments, the Board refused to set up a plaque to the Persons Case as a symbol of women's political equality. It was not until 1998 that the Board agreed to approve a text that reflected such an interpretation; in all likelihood, they acquiesced to feminist historians' arguments concerning the significance of the case both for Canadian women and the British Empire. The life-size statues of the Famous Five that now stand in Calgary's Olympic Plaza and on Parliament Hill are the result of the fundraising efforts of the private Famous 5 Foundation, led by Calgary businesswoman Frances Wright.

If white women were not well represented in state-sponsored commemoration, African-Canadian men and women were even less visible. Between 1957 and 1995, Ontario's plaque program had a very low rate of African-Canadian representation. First began in 1956 by the Archaeological and Historic Sites Board, which was folded into the Ontario Heritage Foundation in 1974, the plaque program for the period initially included only ten (out of a total of 1,000) that commemorated the province's Black history. Out of that ten, three dealt with the early refugee era of the 1770s to the 1840s, while five commemorated the Civil War period. Before the mid-1960s, plaques that dealt with African-Canadian history tended to commemorate white North Americans or British authorities – for example, American abolitionist John Brown and his 1858 convention in Chatham, or British Lieutenant-General John Graves Simcoe's decision to phase out slavery – whose narrative could highlight white activism on behalf of African-Canadians or depict Canada as a haven for Blacks.

After the mid-1960s, the influence of the civil rights movement and of social historians who pointed to African-Canadians' activism played a greater role in determining people, places, or events that would be remembered. Thus, in the 1980s, plaques were put up to honour the early-nineteenth-century Black settlers in the Queen's Bush and to individuals, such as Underground Railroad conductor Harriet Tubman, and Mary Ann Shadd Carey, the Upper Canadian abolitionist, newspaper editor, and lawyer. By 2010, the number of plaques had expanded to twenty-one and included individuals such as William and Susannah Steward, a couple who lived in Niagara in the 1830s and 1840s. The Stewards are remembered for their contribution to the building of the town and for their protection of African-American refugees in the Niagara area.

Plaques and historic sites are not only important markers of the government's and certain groups of Canadians' ideas about what constitutes significant historical events, individuals, and processes; they also have been seen by both governments and private enterprise as helping to play a role in the tourism industry. Not only do the plaques on African-Canadian history remind all Canadians, including those of African descent, about Black communities' long history in the nation, they also have attracted African-American tourists who make a point of visiting these sites in both organized and informal tours.

Plaques, whether commemorating African-Canadians' or others' history, and historic sites such as Louisbourg or Batoche, thus have attempted to reach a broad-based public and educate them about the past in visual and material ways. Museums also have had such goals and, although the history of Canadian museums has received less scholarly attention than that of historic sites, in many ways their founding and development has been similar. Museums in much of British North America tended to be smaller in scale and scope, run by educational and religious institutions and voluntary societies. By the early twentieth century, though, the influence of larger institutions in other major centres, such as Chicago's Field Museum, London's British Museum, and New York's Metropolitan Museum, helped contribute to Torontonians' growing desire for a larger, more impressive institution in their city. While some Ontario residents wanted to see a museum devoted to the province's history, the city's elite called for a comprehensive institution devoted to collections from around the world. Through the efforts of individuals such as Canadian Egyptologist Charles Trick Currelly, collector Sir Edmund Walker, and East Asian specialist George Crofts, and the philanthropic support of Toronto's Massey family, the Royal Ontario Museum (ROM) was founded to provide both educational and moral uplift with its display of items from societies such as Egypt or imperial China. Formally linked to the University of Toronto until 1968, the ROM became an important site for scientific and archaeological work; over the course of the twentieth century, the institution also developed a Canadiana collection.

In contrast to the ROM, Ottawa's National Museum presented more extensive representations of the Canadian past. Created in 1856 as a site in Montreal that displayed minerals, biological specimens, and historical and ethnological artefacts collected by the Geological Survey of Canada, the collection moved to Ottawa in 1881. By the early 1910s, now named the National Museum of Canada, the institution hired prominent anthropologists Edward Sapir, Diamond Jenness, and Marius Barbeau; much of their work focused on acquiring and classifying Indigenous peoples' archaeological remains and artefacts. In these endeavours, the Museum was not alone or unique: over the course of the nineteenth century, a range of collectors had been amassing Indigenous material culture. In Ontario, such efforts included farmers who, in ploughing fields and building homes, had turned up a variety of items that testified to Indigenous occupation and use of the land. They also included those – whether directly connected to academic institutions or involved in voluntary organizations – interested in the anthropological study of Indigenous peoples, groups, and individuals who purposely excavated areas believed to have been Indigenous villages.

Furthermore, collectors from abroad, also influenced by anthropological concepts of North American Indigenous peoples as members of a "dying race" whose material culture needed to be salvaged from the destructive forces of modernity, visited communities in Western Canada and British Columbia, amassing both traditional objects and photographic records of Indigenous communities. To be sure, a number of prominent Indigenous collectors, such as Oronhyatekha, Pauline Johnson, and John Brant-Sero, also participated in these processes, although they did so for a range of reasons, ones which encompassed taking pride in their culture to selling items to institutions and individuals to protect them or to alleviate their own poverty.

If historic sites, then, for much of the twentieth century tended to downplay or ignore Indigenous peoples' multiple and complicated histories, museums and collectors generally saw those histories in anthropological terms, focusing on specimens or artefacts in ways that placed Indigenous people outside of historical narratives, freezing them in time. By the mid-twentieth century, though, institutions such as the ROM or Calgary's Glenbow Museum faced increased challenges from Indigenous people and other groups who felt their histories were misrepresented and that their material culture had been wrongfully appropriated. In response to these concerns, ones which were being expressed by Indigenous groups in a number of countries, a number of Canadian museums thus began to work more closely with communities, sometimes repatriating items to their communities of origin and attempting to incorporate Indigenous knowledge and perspectives into their exhibits.

The Canadian government, then, was not so much a reluctant or unwilling actor in the field of historical commemoration and preservation; rather, its position was complicated by a number of historical contingencies. For one, the federal government's ability to move unilaterally in the preservation and restoration of particular sites, for example, was hampered by provincial, local, and, at times, private jurisdiction; notions of the primacy of private property played no small role in limiting government's powers over heritage designation (a factor that affects heritage designations today). The financial resources needed to undertake large-scale restorations or preservation of sites such as Louisbourg, particularly in the early twentieth century, were often beyond the means of the Canadian state, which in other areas (building railroads, for example) relied on capital supplied by private-sector organizations for public infrastructure. The kinds of cultural policies that eventually helped guide government decision-making were either non-existent or nascent for much of the twentieth century. Furthermore, a general policy was difficult to establish in the face of the divisions that existed between those who wished to commemorate and those who wished to preserve and restore. All of this did not mean that Canadians from across the country felt that government had no role to play in public history. Particularly at the provincial and local levels, politicians sometimes felt besieged by demands that they take responsibility for particular buildings, districts, and sites. At times, provincial governments saw the relationship between "heritage" and tourism as offering a solution to their region's economic woes.

In conclusion, we might return to the examples of other nation-states' involvement with heritage with which this chapter began and ask how the Canadian state's activities have "measured up" against those of Britain and the United States. There are no easy answers to such a question, though. Even quantitative-based responses – the number of historic sites and important provincial and national museums, or the size and budgets of government agencies, for example – would need to be contextualized within the particular cultural, economic, and political histories of those countries, both their histories of historical preservation and the histories that have shaped and influenced the former. After all, comparisons based on sweeping, often very abstract generalizations in which Canada's record is pitted competitively against larger and wealthier nations do not always help us achieve a clearer understanding of historical specificities and complexities. Given Canada's much smaller population and fewer financial resources, it is, perhaps, more remarkable that levels of government and voluntary organizations were engaged in these endeavours. Perhaps the best way to understand this issue is to see where, when, and why various levels of Canadian government took up these questions and to keep in mind the particular historic forces and dynamics that shaped its work.

Historians also, though, need to ask about the wider implications of historic preservation and restoration. Such strategies for promoting history to the public have often favoured more elite or powerful groups whose buildings and material culture either have survived or have been determined more worthy of preservation, not least because more influential individuals or organizations have lobbied for them. The latter were often uninterested in those less prominent, such as servants or workers, whose histories also were part of these sites. While recent efforts at historic preservation have focused on communities such as workers, slaves, free Blacks, or new immigrants, these groups may have left less of a historical "imprint" on the landscape, their homes, workplaces, places of worship, and artefacts more vulnerable to loss, destruction, or deterioration. The state finds it difficult to integrate such histories into its preferred narratives, ones that favour large, sweeping stories of national progress and uplift and that have little room for the histories of marginalized groups.

6

Shaping History through Tourism

Writing to a colleague in the Ontario Historical Society in 1901, the society's secretary David Boyle argued:

There is nothing better calculated to promote patriotism than the honor paid by posterity to those who in the past have served the public. Monuments are not less honorable to those who erect them than to those whom they seek to honor. They are at once an index to the character of a people and constant object lessons of the civic virtues, of heroism, and public and private gratitude. Their educational influence can hardly be overestimated.

Boyle's observations were nothing if not timely, being made in the same year that the province's first monument to Laura Secord at Lundy's Lane was erected. They echo sentiments that, as the previous chapters have shown, were made by numerous commemorators during this period.

But even Boyle believed that monuments offered more than mere lessons in civic consciousness:

There is also a material benefit ... in the added interest that historical sites thus marked acquire in the stimulation of travellers. Hundreds of thousands every year visit the monuments of Europe, and countries possessing such memorials are benefitted pecuniarily to a large extent from these pilgrimages. As an investment, apart altogether from the patriotic side of the questions, the money spent on monuments is a good investment.[1]

"History" thus had the potential to be an economically productive enterprise.

Boyle's quote nicely frames the relationship between the creation of collective memories and histories and the growth of mass tourism. While commemorators often argued that their work was educational in the highest and broadest sense, as it was intended to provide lessons in not just history but civic morality and national identity, they also were aware that monuments and historic sites had the potential to appeal to audiences beyond the local area. This is not meant to suggest that they were insincere concerning those higher goals or that all commemorators believed that attracting tourists was something to which they should aspire. Some local historians, such as Niagara-on-the-Lake's Janet Carnochan, did not appear to have been too concerned about attracting tourists. While happy if tourists came to view historic sites and visited museums, they did not think that historical commemoration existed only to serve a tourist market. HSMBC members certainly were less interested in cultivating a tourist audience. Nevertheless, there were those who believed attracting tourists could serve a number of useful purposes. At a very pragmatic and basic level, entrance and admissions fees might help provide the cash that voluntary organizations needed and that governments did not always supply – monuments, museums, and historic sites did not pay for themselves. Local, regional, provincial, and national boosterism might also motivate the desire to attract tourists. Civic pride and identity could be stimulated by pointing out that important

---

1 David Boyle, "Circular to the Ontario Historical Society," 16 February 1901, Ontario Historical Society Papers, MU5422, Series C, Correspondence, 1898–1903, Archives of Ontario (Toronto).

people, events, and processes occurred in a particular location, and that their historic significance attracted outsiders. Certain landscapes, then, could educate and instruct the public on a number of levels, as well as entertain and amuse visitors from many different areas, possibly even different countries. As historians of culture and leisure have pointed out, mass tourism was one of the most significant developments in Britain, Western Europe, and North America in the mid-nineteenth century. It escalated in importance, culturally, socially, and economically in the twentieth century. Mass tourism was grounded to some extent in the "Grand Tours" of the early modern period, in which aristocratic young men visited Europe's cathedrals, castles, and other historic sites to acquire cultural knowledge and sophistication by appreciating painting and sculpture, gaining an understanding of European history and literature, and developing some degree of competency in French and Italian. At the end of the Napoleonic Wars, entrepreneurs in Belgium developed a brisk trade in battlefield tourism; Waterloo, in particular, began to feature on British tourists' lists of "must-sees." By mid-century, increasing numbers of middle-class tourists began to join their wealthier counterparts, as the introduction of railways, steamships, and English tourism promoter Thomas Cook's package tours aimed at providing a safe, reliable, and instructive experience for novice tourists, particularly middle-class women.

In the North American context, a waterfall was the most sought-after tourist site; it is probably no exaggeration to state that Niagara Falls was the first and most significant tourist attraction in North America. From the end of the War of 1812, the numbers who came to see the Falls grew steadily over the nineteenth century. They came by way of the Erie and Welland Canals (opened in 1825 and 1832, respectively), and the number of bridges and railroads that linked Canada and the United States during the 1840s and 1850s, not to mention the first Atlantic steamship crossings launched in the 1840s. By mid-century, Niagara Falls attracted over 40,000 visitors, who stayed in the hotels that opened on both sides of the border during the 1820s. Until the American Civil War, the Falls was especially popular with southern Americans who came north to escape their home states' intense summer heat. More hotels were built in the 1850s and 1860s and, conscious of their European clientele, hotel managers hired French and German waiters who could both interpret and add a degree of sophistication and cosmopolitan flair to their establishments. Niagara became a North American equivalent of the Grand Tour; those who came to the Falls for its natural beauty would also stop at Boston and Quebec City for these cities' culture and colonial history. The Falls also featured spectacles such as the acrobat Blondin tightrope-walking across it, celebrity tourists, such as the playwright Oscar Wilde, or Aboriginal people selling souvenirs. The presence of Aboriginal people at "historic" tourist sites was both a frequent and complicated phenomenon.

The development of Niagara Falls as a tourist site also included the area's immediate history. American and European visitors who had been visiting battlefields in their own countries were interested in the Niagara peninsula's War of 1812. Often motivated ideologically by romantic notions of the sublime, they welcomed the opportunity to be thrilled, perhaps a little scared, by the natural spectacle of the Falls itself and then moved by the melancholy of battlegrounds. For these – and many others – the emotional experience of historical tourism was a strong attraction. As well, doomed and tragic heroes fascinated these men and women, a passion that found a ready outlet in the figure of General Isaac Brock. His devotion to the people of Upper Canada, his statesmanship, his gallantry in the war, and his reputedly humane treatment of Americans: all of this turned Brock into a very romantic and appealing figure for these visitors.

However, tourists just after the war and in the early 1820s did not have much to guide them in their travels. Except for Brock's monument, few such sites existed, educational plaques had yet to be put up, and only a small number of guidebooks had been written for tourists to consult. Often, tourists had to rely on their own knowledge of the war, as they gazed upon ruined forts and explained the latter's meaning and significance themselves. Those who were guided in their explorations of forts and battlefields were taken around by veterans of the War of 1812 and experienced a combination of partial battle reenactment and oral histories. Their accounts of expeditions to visit Queenston Heights or Lundy's Lane Battleground are full of both the details of the battles fought there and their emotional and sensory dimensions, such as the victors' shouts or the anguished groans of the dying.

By the 1850s, though, both Niagara Falls itself and those who visited it began to change. As the area surrounding the Falls filled up with businesses selling souvenirs and offering a range of experiences linked to the Falls, the waterfall and its environs became a far less mystical and more commodified place. Representations of the Falls started to compete with the "real thing" when, for example, tourists were able to not just stand in front of it and have their picture taken, but could also have a portrait done in a photographers' studio, standing in front of painted backdrop. Tourists thus began to express more scepticism about Niagara Falls; although they continued to arrive, the "sacred" aspect of it gave way to more secular pleasures. As well, although the introduction of a railway line from Chippewa (south Niagara Falls) to Queenston meant that battlefield tourism was still on tourists' itineraries, increasingly there was less and less to see and less meaning to take from a landscape in which ruins were crumbling and becoming less identifiable as specific historic sites. The battleground at Chippewa, for example, dropped off the tourist route.

To be sure, Fort Erie and, in Niagara-on-the-Lake, Fort George retained their romantic charm. Moreover, the Lundy's Lane battleground could still be inspected by the historically inclined tourist. Although partially built over by the growing town of Niagara Falls, tourists could still see the soldiers' graves and, for a fee, climb to the top of a wooden tower built by one of the growing number of tourist promoters and gaze down upon the site. However, Queenston Heights became more popular with tourists for Brock's monument and, in the process, lost much of its mysterious and tragic appeal. By the mid-nineteenth century, visitors tended to drive by the Heights to see the monument from its base but did not stop. Those who did climb down from their carriages usually focused on the monument alone, not the battleground. Judging from their diaries and letters, it was not uncommon for those who climbed the monument's stairs to its top to be overawed by the view of the Niagara River and Lake Ontario, not by the historical significance of the Heights. Historical tourism at Niagara would have to wait until the 1880s and 1890s for its revival.

Not all tourists during this period came to see historic sites. Over the course of the nineteenth century, tourist promoters developed other attractions in Ontario and other parts of Canada that involved recreation, natural beauty, and leisure. Tours up and down the St. Lawrence River were followed by hunting, fishing, and then camping in the Muskoka region north of Toronto; by the end of the century, Muskoka was the most popular destination for leisure holidays in Ontario, followed by places such as Temagami and Algonquin Park. Tourists sought out these areas for their wilderness attractions and for the supposed break they represented from the stresses of modern life, a subject that was increasingly attracting medical and social commentary. By the end of the nineteenth century, doctors and social reformers believed that middle-class men needed to take time away from work to recuperate and to get back to nature. These men were spending the bulk of their time at sedentary jobs, such as clerical and semi-professional occupations in commerce, retail, and government, and no longer worked with their hands or were physically active, a shift that many saw as detrimental to both physical and mental well-being.

Thus, by the early twentieth century, more employers and the cadre of experts in the new field of industrial relations promoted the belief that vacations were necessary for the health of society, which resulted in middle-class professionals receiving paid vacations of one or two weeks. Although working-class people were denied the benefit of annual vacations (not until the 1940s did paid vacation for all workers become accepted and legislated), their employers gradually accepted that they should have a half-day off on Saturday as well as their Sunday day off (because public transit was shut down by municipal authorities on Sunday, working-class people could not enjoy even limited Sunday travel). In Toronto, outings to the Toronto Islands or trips across Lake Ontario to Queenston and Niagara Falls became an increasingly popular form of working-class leisure.

Tourism was not just meant to be entertaining; as in the case of War of 1812 tours, it also could educate sightseers. Travel writers and the tourists themselves believed that looking at historical and cultural sites and landscapes denoted gentility and refinement, the mark of a civilized, cultured, modern Canadian. For middle-class English Canadians, Britain and Western Europe became important international tourist destinations during the late nineteenth century; a number of French Canadians also travelled overseas, often focusing on France. While Canadians had started to go overseas in greater numbers from the 1850s, these grew from the 1870s, as steamships from Quebec City and Halifax increased in both numbers and speed and cheaper second-class tickets made the trip more affordable. These tourists went to see and experience many things. "Nature" certainly played a role – the beauty of the Alps, the breathtaking scenery of the Mediterranean and of the Scottish Highlands, pastoral views of rural England – as did consumption, with clothing from Paris and London's West End, jewellery and glassware from Venice, and perfume from France all being eagerly sought. Moreover, some tourists were interested in industrial attractions, whether they went to see Belfast's and Glasgow's shipyards or Manchester's textile factories. A few went even further afield to tour Greece, the Middle East, and parts of North Africa for cultural, religious, and archaeological reasons. However, the most important and significant reason to go overseas was to experience British and European culture (painting, sculpture, and theatre) and, especially, history. These tourists flocked to places and landscapes they judged to have historic interest and significance such as the Tower of London, Edinburgh Castle, and the historical novelist Walter Scott's home at Abbotsford, Scotland, set up as a historic site and shrine after his death. In Europe, they were intent on seeing Versailles (both for its decor and its past), castles in Germany, and Rome's catacombs. Canada's past was not the only one that educated and enthralled these middle-class Canadians.

Once these tourists returned home, they started to find more options for linking tourism with Canadian history. In Nova Scotia, for example, the establishment of the Dominion-Atlantic Railway in 1894, which used an imagined portrait of the American poet Henry Wadsworth Longfellow's fictional character Evangeline as its figurehead, helped bring masses of tourists to Grand-Pré, eager to find the virtuous maiden in her "forest primeval" and mourn over her sad, yet inspirational, fate. By the 1920s, Canadian roads had improved and automobile tourism began its rise in popularity, a trend that became even more pronounced after the Second World War as the federal government expanded the country's highways. Not only was this seen as an important boost to the Canadian economy, it was also meant to entice Canadians to see more of their country and to draw in American tourist dollars. From the 1880s to the 1940s, auto touring across the United States, particularly to the West and southwest, became a significant part of domestic tourism. American tourism expanded because of

the infrastructure of highways lined with roadside camp-
grounds and motels, and through the development of the
national parks system and the promotion of tourism by the
federal government. Visiting historic sites alongside highways and gazing upon American landscapes was not only
an enjoyable holiday; tourist promoters and the state also
claimed that these activities were part of an American citizen's patriotic duty. Their Canadian counterparts, whether
in government or private enterprise, looked south of the
border and realized the potential of such developments.

The relationship between tourism, history, and the state
was first developed, it seems, most fully in Nova Scotia. As
we have seen, historic societies in that province were highly
visible in the interwar decades in their attempts to preserve and reconstruct historic buildings and sites. Yet along
with the preservation of the architecture and artefacts of
eighteenth- and early-nineteenth-century Loyalists, another
history of the province was being written, crafted by native-
born Maritimers such as folklorist Helen Creighton, and
more recent arrivals to the province, such as handcrafts
promoter and educator Mary Black. Creighton, a journalist from Dartmouth, became fascinated with the songs and
stories produced by the province's rural and, in particular, fishing communities. After receiving formal academic
training in the United States, Creighton was able to secure
funding from the federal government (through contracts
with the Ottawa-based National Museum of Canada) and
from the province to travel around Nova Scotia and collect
"folklore." The province circulated her published writings
of folktales in its elementary schools and her books became
best-sellers. Creighton's work, along with that of other writers and provincial promoters, was directed at both Nova
Scotia's residents and the tourist market, the latter seen by
the provincial government in the interwar decades as the
salvation of an economy whose industry had crumbled just
after the First World War. Creighton's efforts were complemented in 1940s by those of Mary Black, who was hired by

the provincial Department of Education to spearhead a crafts revival to develop industry in rural areas and to bring in tourists. Black's work, though, often involved teaching rural women new craft practices that were thought to be more attractive for the tourist market, frequently overriding existing techniques or asserting notions of long-standing craft traditions that were non-existent.

The handcrafts "revival" also went well with Creighton's writings, ones that created an image of Nova Scotia as a haven of innocence, a place where the "simple life," removed from the stresses and strains of modernity, could be found. While such depictions might seem harmless to outsiders, they were often patronizing, since they tended to paint Nova Scotians as not only living a "simple life" but being somewhat simple, quaint, and backwards themselves. The type of "histories" created by such tourist promoters also denied Nova Scotians their actual histories, substituting instead homogenous images of people frozen in a time that had little connection to real historical events and processes. Creighton's work relied on ideas about racial essences or "types" to explain problems such as persistent poverty, underdevelopment, or dangerous workplaces. Fishermen of the province's South Shore, for example, were seen as hardy types drawn by the allure of the sea who clung to a romantic and thrilling way of life that, despite its perils, they did not wish to change, a depiction that ignored their attempts to do something about dangerous working conditions through high attrition rates and attempts to organize unions. Nova Scotians were also said to be highly superstitious people. Creighton's collection of stories about magic and the occult, *Bluenose Ghosts* (1957) and *Bluenose Magic: Popular Beliefs and Superstitions in Nova Scotia* (1966), sold well and were used in the province's schools to teach children about their past. Rather than exploring the social, political, and cultural foundations for such beliefs, though, Creighton's work depicted Nova Scotians as shunning science and established religion in favour of cures for witches, visions, or premonitions. Such images ignored the province's history of many institutions of higher education, scientific and rational thought, and multiple religious denominations.

Seeing the province as the place of the "folk" also denied the presence and histories of African–Nova Scotians and Aboriginal people. In Nova Scotian travel and fiction writer Will R. Bird's books, for example, Yorkshiremen who had settled in Nova Scotia tended to possess heaping amounts of good character, while Blacks and Aboriginals generally tended to be woefully lacking in it, displaying atavistic qualities of childishness or primitive savagery. Thomas R. Raddall's popular historical novels, set primarily in eighteenth-century Nova Scotia, also used concepts of gender, race, and class to describe his characters, concepts that relied on notions of racial and gender hierarchy. In Raddall's narratives of the province's history, Anglo-Celtic men were superior, women of all races and classes were suspected of being sexually promiscuous and a threat to men's morality, and all other races were degenerate (African–Nova Scotians, First Nations). Moreover, Europeans having too much contact with the latter might result in the former also becoming degenerate. Raddall believed that the French in Acadia, for example, owed their downfall not to their subjugation to the British but to their intermingling with the Mi'kmaq, an interracial alliance which left them too soft and weak to withstand British attacks.

Instead of being a province with a complicated, sometimes confusing, history of multiple ethnic and linguistic groups, Nova Scotia was to become not just the province of the "folk" – it also was an enclave of Scottishness. The provincial premier, Angus L. Macdonald, was eager to promote the (erroneous) notion that the Scots formed the majority of the province's population. The province went so far as to create a tartan for Nova Scotia, the first Canadian province to do so, and stationed a bagpiper wearing the plaid at the Nova Scotia-New Brunswick border to welcome tourists. According to Macdonald and his supporters, Scottish immigrants had given the province its distinct identity, one supposedly grounded in the "rugged individualism" of the Highlands. It was also a decidedly white identity and other groups, such as Aboriginals, were deemed as being of lesser importance or inconsequential to the province's past. As well as exaggerating the predominance of people of Scots descent in Nova Scotia, this myth of "Scottishness" glossed over the ways in which particular historical processes – the Highland clearances, English colonialism, and unequal socio-economic relations within Scotland – were responsible for the Scottish presence in Nova Scotia. The province also was ambivalent about the most highly visible manifestation of the Scots' presence, the Gaelic language. While Macdonald venerated Gaelic, like Creighton and the fishing communities of the South Shore, he tended to idealize and mystify it, treating the language as part of the great romance of Scottishness but consigning it to a distant past (the fact that he was far from fluent in Gaelic did not help). Despite the demands of prominent Gaelic speakers, such as Sydney's James MacNeil, that it be taught as a living language in the province's schools and that Gaelic broadcasting be defended, the province's response was, at best, half-hearted. The Gaelic College at St. Ann's, for example, did little more than promote a de-historicized and romantic "Scottishness" embodied in craft classes, a gift shop full of souvenirs, and annual summer festivities designed to celebrate notions of "traditional clan" hierarchies and, not incidentally, attract tourists.

Nova Scotians, though, were not alone in such self-representation. American writers and tourist promoters saw New England, especially Nantucket, as a place in which the supposed values of colonial America could be found. Rural independence, class harmony, and a supposedly simple and more virtuous life were the hallmarks of Nantucket and its "pure Yankee" descendants, not to mention the production of colonial handicrafts. However, Nantucket was a commercial area in decline; its residents were well-travelled, its history one in which conflict was a familiar phenomenon, and, as a whaling centre, its residents were of mixed ethnic and racial backgrounds: Portuguese, South Sea Islanders, Aboriginals, and African-Americans. Nevertheless, as in the case of Nova Scotia, these ways of seeing a landscape and understanding the place of history in it were powerful. They were created when local and regional economies needed some form of rejuvenation and middle-class outsiders were being advised that such nostalgic enclaves would meet their moral, spiritual, and cultural needs. Moreover, stereotypes of Nova Scotia as a land of the fisherfolk, or of Nantucket as a haven of Yankee independence, possessed just enough kernels of truth to make them plausible; the fact that there were other histories of these areas became lost in the desire to find the "authentic" tourist experience.

Creighton and Black were far from being alone in their interest in the songs, tales, and material culture of "the folk" in Canada, nor were they the first to collect such material. The work of Marius Barbeau, the Quebec-born anthropologist who had trained under the noted German-American scholar Franz Boas, has been credited with preserving a number of French-Canadian songs. Born in 1883 in Ste-Marie-de-Beauce, Quebec, Barbeau's research interests took him initially to the Pacific Northwest Coast, where he studied Aboriginal peoples' totemic systems. Barbeau then moved to the Huron community of Lorette in Quebec, to conduct work for the Geological Survey of Canada; there he was struck by French-Canadian influences on Aboriginal songs performed by the community's elders. Encouraged by Boas, Barbeau embarked on a career of fieldwork, travelling by boat and bicycle throughout the province so that he might record songs performed by both Aboriginal people and elderly French Canadians. Although he began publishing those songs in the academic journal called *Journal of American Folklore*, in 1916, Barbeau became convinced that these songs needed to be more widely shared with the

Canadian public. He saw them as the cultural essence of Quebec, a pure distillation of its spirit that was untouched by modernity. In 1919, he staged a demonstration in Montreal that involved folk singers, dancers, and storytellers, who performed on a stage dressed as the interior of a rural French-Canadian home. His *Folk Songs of Modern Canada* was published in 1925 and was followed by a number of other, smaller-scale books. During his career, Barbeau collected 13,000 texts and recorded 7,000 melodies; in his capacity as director of the National Museum, he also worked to promote Quebec and French-Canadian handicrafts, games, art, and architecture.

Unlike Creighton and Black, though, Barbeau was less interested in promoting his province's folk culture and material history for the benefit of tourists, as he saw the latter as damaging the purity of French-Canadian culture. Yet Quebec also had a "history" of being seen by visitors as a retreat into a less complex, undemanding time – in its case, either that of the rural seventeenth century or the heroic and romantic days of New France (the latter often typified by Quebec City or the older quarter of Montreal). Late-nineteenth-century historians such as Lionel Groulx and François-Xavier Garneau liked to point to travellers' observations of "folk" culture in New France, evidence that these historians thought demonstrated the kind of purity they, and Barbeau, prized. By the mid-twentieth century, the province was visited by a number of American, English-Canadian, and French-Canadian travel writers who came prepared to see the "historic" Quebec whose images they had gleaned from novels, history texts and readers, or films. In particular, the very popular novel *Maria Chapdelaine*, written by the French author Louis Hémon (1880–1913), played an important role for English-Canadian tourists. Published posthumously in French in 1916 and then translated into English in 1921, the novel, set in the early twentieth century in Quebec's Lac-St-Jean region (several hundred kilometres north of Quebec City) where Hémon lived for a short time, supposedly captured agrarian French-Canadian life. Its central character, Maria Chapdelaine, chooses to remain in the area instead of migrating to New England, declaring "in this land of Quebec nothing has changed. Nor shall anything change, for we are the pledge of it." Such images, promising timeless and stable "folkways," played a significant role in shaping tourists' expectations and desires.

Even as textbooks of the post-Second World War years began to discuss "modern" Quebec – stressing, for example, economic and agricultural progress – anglophone travel writers still arrived with the notion that historic rural French-Canadian culture and contemporary Quebec lifestyles were the same; they wanted to see *habitants* living like their ancestors, not to mention producing the same crafts. French-Canadian writers also relied on such assumptions, although usually to offer these archetypes as role models to be emulated for their moral virtues and religious beliefs. Although they did so for different reasons, these groups participated in a broader national cultural practice, that of seeing the habitant as a pre-modern, unspoiled, happy being, who lived just as his seventeenth-century ancestors in Normandy had and who thus provided a soothing antidote to the stresses and strains of modern life. To be sure, English-Canadian writers also seized on signs of industrial growth, particularly in Montreal, as evidence of Quebec's progress and promising future. However, the provincial government responded to most of the travel writing by promoting Quebec as a province of history and, through the Department of Agriculture and rural women's groups, folk crafts.

By the 1940s, the province began to insist that habitants and "Old Quebec" were not the only attractions: Quebec also offered modern and up-to-date contemporary attractions, such as Montreal's urban sophistication. Moreover, between the 1880s and 1950s, rural French Canadians actively sought out urban material and incorporated it into their songs and dances; those who migrated to Montreal or Maine, for example, might bring back new words, tunes, and steps. By the 1950s, communities began to replace the regular and informal practice of meeting in each other's homes for dancing and singing with more formally organized events in hotels and village halls. As well, ballroom dancing, taught by outside instructors, began to grow in popularity; traditional dances such as the *gigue* became rarer. However, in the 1970s, other programs and events helped to reinforce and, in some ways, recreate the province's image as a haven of folk culture. The *Vacance-Familles,* in which tourists stayed as paying guests with rural families in areas such as the Beauce, Gaspé, Eastern Townships, or Kamouraska, was one such initiative. Often farming families who might be struggling to make a living from the land, these rural hosts invited tourists to participate in traditional events such as the Christmas Eve *réveillon,* a celebration held after Midnight Mass which featured feasting, card-playing, and dancing. Yet in many cases these communities had revived "traditional" gatherings, motivated by the presence of tourists and 1970s Quebec nationalism. In one case, a Beauce community interrupted their own *réveillon* to watch a Radio-Canada broadcast of a staged version in which they had participated a few weeks earlier. The same community had seen a decline in traditional dancing until their village celebrated its 300th anniversary; the residents' renewed interest in these dances was sparked by television broadcasters' invitations to perform them for its audience. As well, larger-scale celebrations – 1970s Christmas craft fairs in Montreal and Quebec City, a staged exhibit of dancing, singing, and storytelling at the latter's Winter Carnival in 1978, and other seasonal celebrations – told of a revival of folk practices and material culture for audiences both within and outside of the province.

Others found ideas about folk culture useful, although they might use them in somewhat different ways. Between 1928 and 1931, journalist and Canadian Pacific Railway

advertising agent John Murray Gibbon (who also was fascinated by the history of the Scots in Canada) staged sixteen
folk music and handicrafts festivals across Canada. Gibbon,
born in Ceylon (Sri Lanka) to Scottish parents and educated
at the Universities of Aberdeen and Oxford, was drawn to
ideas about folk culture in the writings of Jean-Jacques Rousseau and Rousseau's German contemporary, Johann Got-
tfried von Herder; their work convinced Gibbon that folk
traditions were great national treasures and should be collected, preserved, and displayed. Gibbon began his career
as a promoter of the folk in 1925 by organizing a series of
concerts of French-Canadian folk songs, performed by the
well-known French-Canadian folksinger Charles Marchand.
Held at Quebec City's Château Frontenac, Marchand's performances were so successful that they inspired Gibbon to
translate and publish Marchand's more popular songs and
launch the New Canadian Folk Song and Handicraft Festival, held in Winnipeg, Regina, and Calgary. First featuring
Eastern European and, then, "other racial groups" from
Europe, in 1928 the festival expanded to include British
and French Canadians. It included concerts of song and
dance that were accompanied by demonstrations of "Folk"
crafts and textiles, such as embroidery, leatherwork, carving, pottery, handwoven cloth, and beadwork.

   Despite Gibbon's inclusion of English, Scottish, Welsh,
Irish, and French-Canadian groups in these festivals, which
might suggest that all were on an equal footing, he struc-
tured the program so that their contributions were seen
as those of two founding nations, English and French, and
were the most important. Gibbon saw the traditions of
other European groups as interesting and enjoyable but
also as less central to notions of Canada's heritage, while
he rarely promoted the cultural practices of Aboriginal,
Metis, and African-Canadians (and in some cases, did not
represent them at all). At the 1930 festival held at Calgary's Palliser Hotel, the event began with a pageant that
staged a tableau called "Western Canada" that featured

"Old-Timers," pioneers from Britain or Eastern Canada, North-West Mounted Police officers, missionaries, ranchers, cowboys, and the Sarcee people. The accompanying narrative claimed that these "Canadian pioneers, French and British" (along with those few Aboriginals left in the region) had "settled" the area and laid the important foundation for newer arrivals, such as Eastern Europeans. To be sure, Gibbon's motivations appear to have been primarily nationalistic and not to promote tourism as an economic panacea. He wished to find a way of incorporating new Canadians into the Canadian nation while simultaneously preserving their cultural traditions (and those of British and French Canadians). Although we do not know the extent to which tourists composed Gibbon's audiences, the railway had played a central part in bringing tourists to Western Canada and British Columbia, drawn to attractions such as the Rocky Mountains, Vancouver, and Victoria, as well as steamship excursions up the Pacific Northwest Coast. Like industrial and commercial exhibitions, it may well have been that the festivals, advertised by Gibbon in major Western newspapers, attracted both city residents and outsiders.

Ideas about the importance of folk culture, particularly its oral transmission through twentieth-century media, also might be found in 1930s Newfoundland. Like Nova Scotia, the island also had its own collectors of folk songs and stories; one of the most prominent members of this group was Newfoundland businessman Gerald S. Doyle. Based in St. John's, Doyle distributed American and Canadian goods, along with his own brand of cod liver oil. He also was an avid collector of folk songs from Newfoundland's coastal communities and was interested in contemporary composers who used traditional forms, such as Otto Kelland, the author of *Let Me Fish Off Cape St. Mary's*. Doyle published the *Gerald S. Doyle Song Book* (which also ran advertisements for his cod liver oil) and hosted a popular radio show on the Newfoundland Broadcasting Corporation station, the *Gerald S. Doyle New Bulletin*, which featured a mixture of local

news and announcements. Doyle's counterpart in broadcasting, journalist and future premier Joseph R. Smallwood,
began his career as a folk historian in 1937 by writing down
folk narratives and tales for a St. John's newspaper. Later
that year he moved to radio, where he broadcast the *Barrelman* program. On the *Barrelman*, Smallwood recounted
narratives from the island's oral folk culture that he had
collected, with the aim of promoting Newfoundland culture as a means of encouraging patriotism (and promoting
himself as a nationalistic leader). While Smallwood was not
above recounting "tall tales" that a number of his listeners
felt lacked credibility, historians have pointed out that his
stories of Newfoundlanders stressed their ability to withstand adversity, demonstrate courage, and endure the hard-
ships of the Depression with stoicism, a kind of self-help
that might inspire Newfoundlanders. From 1943 to 1955,
the program was hosted by journalist Michael Harrington,
who chose longer, more factually based items. Using the
modern media of radio, then, Doyle and Smallwood helped
create popular cultural icons based in folk history.

Such icons, it seems, were not created directly for tourist
audiences, though, as the radio broadcasts were aimed at listeners within Newfoundland. While tourism in Newfoundland was linked to the island's residents, this was done in a
somewhat different manner. Tourism and its relationship to
constructions of the island's past were shaped by Newfoundland's late-nineteenth-century history of out-migration and
a desire of residents, particularly those concerned with economic development, to bring those émigrés back, if only
for a short time. Although Newfoundland had its share of
late-nineteenth-century tourism organized around hunting
and fishing, Old Home Weeks became very popular, first
staged in 1904 when 600 ex-residents attended the gathering. These events continued into the 1920s and, although
halted by the Depression and the Second World War, they
rose in popularity again in the postwar years. By the 1960s,
the provincial government's Tourist Development Board

had become heavily involved in the promotion of these weeks and, in 1966, the province ran a celebration of the Smallwood government's legacy called "Come Home Year." Designed to attract both ex-Newfoundlanders and tourists, the province promoted the nostalgia that the former might feel, based in childhood memories of home and family. It also promoted modern improvements that made travel around the island easier for both former residents and tourists, including the completion of the Trans-Canada Highway across its interior, improved ferry services, provincial parks, and a network of roads that allowed visits to the outports by car. Field workers were sent out to advise residents on how to be helpful and welcoming to the expected visitors. The province also reissued Boyle's book of folksongs and published a raft of promotional literature (including new maps), license plates, and songs.

Notions of "the folk" were not the only means of linking history and tourism, though. In 1939, Prince Edward Island celebrated the Charlottetown Conference's seventy-fifth anniversary, an event that provides insight into both the relationship between tourism and commemoration and federal-provincial interactions in these processes. In the 1930s, tourism promoters of the island focused on its pastoral attractions and the figure of Anne of Green Gables (as they still do today). However, by deciding to highlight the anniversary of the Conference for the entire month of July, Island boosters also claimed a significant national role for it in Canadian history. The Prince Edward Island Publicity Association, an organization formed in the 1920s, argued that promoting the anniversary with large-scale provincial events would raise awareness of the Island within Canada and internationally. They also believed that bringing the federal government into these celebrations would go some way to healing the rifts between it and the provinces that developed during the 1930s over the handling of relief programs. To these commemorators, the Charlottetown Conference seemed like a perfect opportunity to promote such harmonious relations: it did not involve battles, claims, and disputes (or at least not as they represented it). Rather, they could depict the Conference as embodying a common vision of Canada's future.

To be sure, the organizers were less successful than they had hoped in enticing the most prominent federal figures; neither Prime Minister Mackenzie King nor Governor General Lord Tweedsmuir, for example, attended. Nevertheless, with both provincial and federal financial support, they successfully managed to combine historical elements with a number of other events. The Conference itself was marked by the unveiling of Historic Sites and Monuments Board plaques that commemorated the Fathers of Confederation, a historic parade with 2,000 participants, and a lavish pageant, the *Romance of Canada*, that featured eighty performers, an eighty-person chorus, a twenty-piece orchestra, and drew 8,000 spectators. Although D.C. Harvey, an Island native and head of the HSMBC, grumbled that the real anniversary of the Conference was September, not July (the organizers chose July because September's weather was less predictable and it would conflict with the fall harvest and provincial exhibition), he was persuaded to take a prominent role in the plaque ceremonies, which also were broadcast nationally on CBC radio. As well, the event's organizers treated visitors and residents to public celebrations that included yacht races, choral performances, the inauguration of the Charlottetown airport and Royal Canadian Air Force flyovers, a Carnival Queen contest, followed by a Mardi Gras parade and carnival, and military exercises.

According to the Island's newspapers, thousands of tourists were attracted to the events of July 1939. Such an influx of visitors must have pleased the organizers, whose promotional efforts included 5,000 brochures sent across the Maritimes, Maine, and Quebec, and an additional 100,000 circulated at New York City's 1939 World Fair, advertisements placed in Eastern Canadian and northeastern U.S. newspapers, 20,000 booklets, films shown at service clubs across Canada, and luggage and automobile labels. Overall, the celebrations achieved the organizers' goals. Island residents and the provincial government, eager to show off their province, were satisfied with such well-attended historical and popular events; the federal government was able to promote tourism, take credit for economic development, and champion national unity. Moreover, although the memory of the 1939 celebration itself – like that of the 1908 Champlain Tercentenary – was for many Canadians fleeting, the celebration identified Prince Edward Island as more than just a pleasant tourist destination. It also could claim to be a national shrine, one set apart from other, similar regions because of its role in Confederation, a province that deserved national (and tourist) attention because of its worthiness as the site of a national, historic event. Furthermore, in the early 1960s, the 1939 celebration proved to be a template that organizers of the 100th anniversary of the Conference drew upon, although they did so on a far grander scale. The celebrations of 1964 ran for the entire year; $5 million went to the construction of the Confederation Centre, and in 1973, the provincial legislature at which the 1864 Conference was held became part of Parks Canada's historic sites.

If the Atlantic provinces, Quebec, and Western Canada have been important sites in which to study the relationships between historical preservation, concepts of tradition and folk, and tourism, First Nations peoples in Canada have, it could be argued, been an important "site" themselves in which these cultural and social processes have played out. An interest in Aboriginal people, of course, predates the rise of modern tourism or the late-nineteenth-century historic preservation movement. Accounts written by early modern travellers to North America invariably mentioned sightings of and encounters with Indigenous people; the latter also recorded their own perceptions and representations of Europeans. By the early nineteenth century, at places such as Niagara Falls and Kahnawake, near Montreal, Iroquoian women found a market for their beadwork and baskets among travellers and settlers, eager to purchase souvenirs that would serve as reminders of their travels and of those who had crafted the items. At one point, historians saw these exchanges as proof that Aboriginal culture had become degraded by exposure to whites because of the women's use of European motifs and materials and thus denigrated the souvenirs as early examples of "tackiness" or "kitsch." However, more recently scholars of material culture have pointed out that they represented an important example of cross-cultural contact, as they merged Aboriginal traditions and practices with new cultural forms and materials. Similar developments occurred on the Pacific Northwest Coast.

Over the course of the nineteenth century, Aboriginal people in Canada were eager to present their own narratives of their history, pre- and post-contact, in pageants, parades, and, in some cases, in historical societies. When possible, they also appeared at tourist sites, partly because of the economic opportunities these sites offered when Aboriginal people were being squeezed out of industry, commerce, and agriculture, and partly because these sites offered a chance for them to represent their history. To be sure, these appearances were not without problems, since tourists often arrived expecting to see not Iroquois or Mi'kmaq people but, rather, a war bonneted male Plains Indian, an image that, thanks to advertising and television, became ubiquitous by the mid-twentieth century. In 1976, for example, organizers of the Olympics' closing ceremony in Montreal featured Plains Indians and tepees, an odd and rather awkward way of including Aboriginal people in its representations of Canada. As well, tourists often saw the residents of Indian villages, Aboriginal performers, and souvenir vendors as remnants of a dying race, believing that few "real Indians" were left in Canada. Those that did exist inhabited, like the folk, pre-modern time and lived apart from modern technology and institutions, being more like museum specimens than actual human beings.

However, at times Indigenous peoples' work at tourist sites could have political significance. In the 1920s, for example, when the U.S. government passed legislation that abrogated the Aboriginal right enshrined in the Jay Treaty to cross the U.S.-Canada border freely, the Tuscarora leader Clinton Rickards used his appearances in Aboriginal clothing at Niagara Falls' tourist camps as a means of gathering support for Aboriginal opposition to the law (which was repealed). As well, First Nations' involvement in the Indian Pavilion at Expo 67 marked an important shift or turning point in their representation for home and tourist audiences. Even though the federal government generally wished to demonstrate that the history of Indigenous-newcomer relations was one of the former's assimilation to the latter's values and practices, First Nations participants presented a more nuanced message and pushed spectators to consider more carefully the effect of colonization on Aboriginal people. While the Pavilion suggested that Aboriginal and non-Aboriginal Canadian histories were intertwined – for the most part, harmoniously – it also made it quite clear that that harmony had come about because of Aboriginal munificence and that the latter had paid a very high price in this exchange.

One of the most highly visible places in which Indigenous people represent their history for today's tourists is the historic site, in locations such as Sainte-Marie-among-the-Hurons, Old Fort William in northwestern Ontario, and Lower Fort Garry in Manitoba. These institutions have added Indigenous interpreters who come from a range of tribal groups as a means of providing Aboriginal perspectives that contradict the "traditional" narratives of triumphal European expansion and settlement. To be sure, these interpreters face challenges similar to those of their ancestors, as they encounter predominantly non-Aboriginal audiences that are frequently ignorant about Aboriginal histories and have a sense of the past shaped by Hollywood westerns, novels, the news, and romantic stereotypes of Aboriginal peoples (typically conflated with the Plains people). Indigenous interpreters, however, have developed their own educational strategies to deal with attitudes and comments that range from clumsy, albeit well-meaning ones, to extremely racist notions of "savages." For one, they see themselves as representatives of their respective communities and make a point of educating themselves in their histories, which for them are not something distant or "over and done with" but, rather, affect their contemporary lives in myriad ways (e.g., dealing with the Indian Act). Those histories are then brought into their ongoing, daily interactions with tourist audiences, as the interpreters correct inaccurate assumptions with answers and comments designed to provide concrete information about Aboriginal peoples' lives, beliefs, and material culture. Visitors who make derogatory statements about Aboriginal people are directly confronted by the interpreters, who tease them about their ignorance or insist that they stop using offensive words and phrases (such as "squaw" or "how") while also informing them why particular words are objectionable, how they happened to be used, and what the correct phrase or behaviour is. Although the weight of popular images of First Nations people is enormous, having as it does a very long and powerful history of its own, the Indigenous interpreters' creativity and ingenuity suggests that tourism might present more educational opportunities than we might assume.

To return to David Boyle's argument that tourism might help promote awareness of the past: was he correct? Could there have been a "right" mixture of balance for state, historical preservation, and tourism, one in which the interests of tourist promoters came second to a more complex vision of the past? There are no easy or clear-cut answers to such a question. For one, the government's interest and interventions in the connections between tourism and history might have led to a vision of a region's past that was retrogressive and denied complexity and conflict, as a way of securing historic tourism as part of future regional economic development. In the case of Nova Scotia, such a situation had implications beyond the realm of tourism, as it helped lay the blame for the region's economic problems on the shoulders of its populace's "natural" tendencies. Moreover, when governments lacked fiscal resources to develop sites, or believed in the sanctity of private property, tourist entrepreneurs might prove all too ready to step in with their own particular visions of what "the past" might look like. Strategies for attracting tourists, then, helped shape local approaches to history and thus limited the kinds of historical narratives told about particular places. Tourism also, though, might provide economic opportunities and audiences for those who lacked access to resources and political clout in other realms. If practised within contexts in which such groups enjoyed at least a degree of control over the way in which their histories were represented, it might open up possibilities for education – their own and that of outsiders. Such dilemmas persist into the early twenty-first century, indicating that nineteenth- and early-twentieth-century tourism has left a powerful legacy.

7

Teaching the Nation Its History: Schoolchildren and the Canadian Past

Monuments, museums, parades, pageants, and written texts have been important public artefacts of commemoration, their creation by both voluntary groups and levels of government illustrative of the complexities of creating public memories and histories. These activities and the narratives they told were aimed at audiences that included a range of social groups, audiences that incorporated both men and women and, at times, cut across significant divisions of region, language, ethnicity, and race. Yet another important group in these activities was Canadian children. Although children, both as participants in and targets of commemoration, have received less focused attention in the scholarship on public history in Canada, historians' research shows nevertheless that they were present in many commemorative activities. Children appeared in dedication ceremonies when monuments were unveiled; they acted in pageants, recited poetry, and sang hymns and anthems at Remembrance Day ceremonies; and they were taken to museums and historic sites by their teachers, gradually becoming a significant part of these institutions' programs. Those who organized commemorations often focused on children directly: they might ask them to write essays about the particular meaning of an event or person, for example, or encourage them to fundraise for monuments or memorial sites. Empire Day celebrations in Ontario, for example, centred on the spectacle of children singing and reciting speeches and poetry or acting in historical pageants. Schools themselves were often used to memorialize individuals or events, whether linked to the heroic age of New France, battles and generals of the War of 1812 or the First World War, and Western explorers and prominent "pioneers." Moreover, it was probably no accident or coincidence that a number of local historians and commemorators, such as Niagara's Janet Carnochan, were – or had been – teachers.

Equally significantly, as history developed as an academic discipline in late-nineteenth-century Canadian universities, both English and French, it also became a more important subject in the country's schools. Beginning in the 1890s, history became compulsory, a subject that students had to take alongside English or mathematics; they also could study Canadian history at the upper elementary level and at junior and senior levels in high school. Younger students, thought by educators not yet ready to study history as a separate subject, might learn lessons about the past in stories printed in readers and biographies in which children could learn about select individuals in Canadian history, an important aspect of history education since not all of Canada's youth went on to enter, let alone complete, high school until the interwar decades, and far fewer did so in rural areas. It was not until the 1960s, with significant increases in high school enrolments, changing ideas about pedagogy, and concerns about the perceived narrow focus of the curriculum, that history lost its privileged status.

The reasons for history taking a central role in the school curriculum were bound up with nineteenth-century understandings of its link to national identities and the need to foster ideals of citizenship. In a country such as Canada, which by the 1890s saw its electoral franchise expand to include the majority of its male citizenry, public education of the latter (and eventually, of their female counterparts) was seen by politicians and educators as crucial to combat illiteracy and ill-informed choices. These lessons that were often tied to learning about the nation's history were not overly controversial, yet different groups of Canadians agreed that knowledge of the country's past was immensely useful in making sound decisions about its future.

To be sure, such knowledge was far from neutral or without political import. In Quebec, from the mid-nineteenth century on, the "Heroic Period" (1534–1663) of New France's history became popular in teaching history to schoolchildren. As Quebec intellectuals became increasingly worried about changes to the province – industrialization, rural migration (both within Quebec and to New England), and urbanization – portraits of New France's earliest years could serve as a lesson for a society undergoing such changes. By stressing the virtues of rural life, "heroic" figures such as Dollard des Ormeaux and Champlain, and, above all, the dominance of the Roman Catholic Church, historians such as abbé Henri-Raymond Casgrain believed that history might offer a guide so that their students would withstand and resist such changes. Such historians also attributed a role to divine providence and the colonists' (particularly missionaries') moral superiority in their ability to withstand Aboriginal attacks on New France. Quebec was far from the only province in which history lessons served a number of moral and political purposes, though. From the 1890s until at least the interwar decades, teaching English-speaking Canadians about their past almost invariably meant teaching them about Canada's ties to Britain. Events such as the coming of the Loyalists, for example, or the War of 1812, were highlighted by educators as significant because they illustrated an ongoing history of loyalty to Britain and the Empire. In English Canada, departments of education aimed such lessons – the dominance of the English language, the superiority of Canadian political institutions because of their link to British traditions, and the history of Canada as a tale of progress and prosperity – at those Protestant Canadians of British descent and at those whose loyalty might be suspect, such as Mennonites, Doukhobors, Catholics, and recently arrived immigrants from southern and Eastern Europe. First Nations students, whether in residential or day schools, were reminded by their teachers of the historical ascendancy of Europeans over their ancestors, a lesson that was underscored by the efforts of both church and state to eradicate Aboriginal languages and cultural practices (although on the Six Nations' reserve near Brantford, Ontario, a number of Aboriginal teachers in the day schools, often women, told children about their histories and culture). Working-class Canadians, politicians and educators believed, also needed to be told of the superiority of the country's political and economic institutions, particularly if they belonged to left-wing organizations. For educators and politicians, events such as the 1919 Winnipeg General Strike and labour unrest in the Maritimes needed to be countered with narratives of the rise of Canadian capitalism and parliamentary democracy.

Like monuments and historic paintings, history textbooks indicate their authors' interpretations and conceptions of the past; they are also significant artefacts of historical commemoration, produced by both conflict and consensus. In Quebec, as previously mentioned, the early years of New France played a major role in French-language history lessons. An important theme of these narratives was the clash between the French and Indigenous people who, starting in the mid-nineteenth century, were portrayed as "Le Sauvage," noted for their warlike tendencies, treachery, cruelty, superstitious nature, and lack of social order and discipline. The exception to this stereotype were the Huron, allies of the French, whose defeat at the hands of the Iroquois was depicted as a battle between the forces of good and evil. That both communities belonged to the same cultural and linguistic group was either unknown or ignored by historians who wrote in this vein, as were Iroquois motives for waging war with the Huron, or the latter's exposure to European diseases. Only conversion to Catholicism could transform Indigenous people, turning them into peaceful, well-behaved residents of the colony who were no longer a threat to its security. In these texts, then, Aboriginal people became foils for French valour and tenacity, as they provided the setting in which these qualities might be displayed and carried out.

Such representations continued well into the twentieth century. Paul-Emile Farley and Gustave Lamarche's *Histoire du Canada,* which from its first publication in 1934 until the 1960s was the textbook used in most of Quebec's French-language secondary school history classes, depicted Aboriginal people as warlike, immoral, treacherous, and superstitious. In other history textbooks, though, such as those written by Jean Bruchési and Albert Tessier in the 1940s and 1950s, Indigenous people began to disappear from their narratives. As well, the rise of a new group of university-based textbook writers in the post-Second World War period, ones influenced by other historiographic trends, meant that history teaching at the secondary level began to focus less on the "Heroic Period" and more on the British Conquest of 1759. The exceptions to this practice – Gustave Lanctot and Marcel Trudel – depicted Aboriginal people as initially friendly towards Europeans; they acted as guides and introduced them to new forms of technology and food essential to their survival in the colony. However, such works were unable to understand Aboriginal cultures in their own right and context or to include the thousands of years of Indigenous history before European contact.

English-language texts had their own particular stories to tell. From the 1870s to the 1930s, textbooks published in Ontario, where the majority of English-language textbooks were produced in those decades, provided descriptions of New France and Acadia but tended to agree that the most important foundational events in "Canada's" history were the arrival of the Loyalists and the War of 1812. Although a number of textbooks discussed the establishment of "pioneer society," the building of towns, the coming of the railroads, and other aspects of social and economic history, politics and warfare dominated the books of the late nineteenth and early twentieth century. Moreover, their writers insisted that the War of 1812 had been a turning point in the development of the Canadian nation, notwithstanding the fact that it had not affected the British North American colonies equally. Readers of Charles G.D. Roberts's 1905 *History of Canada for High Schools and Academies*, for example, were told that the deaths and destructions brought by the war "were not too great a price to pay for the bond of brotherhood between the scattered provinces. The bond of brotherhood that then first made itself felt, from Cape Breton to the Straits of Mackinaw, grew secretly but surely in power till it proclaimed itself to the world in Confederation, and reached out to the islands of the Pacific."[1]

Although some authors admitted that the war was triggered by international and imperial conflicts over which the colonists had little control and little initial interest, they all agreed that the threat of American invasion was met with bravery and determination to keep the colony "British" (and, thus, ultimately Canadian). The narrative of the war was one of masculine heroism, patriotism, resistance, and self-sacrifice, exemplified by the death of General Isaac Brock at Queenston Heights but also found in the behaviour of the militia. While a number of writers acknowledged the support of Aboriginal allies and were generally quite flattering in their description of the Shawnee leader Tecumseh, Indigenous people tended to disappear from the Ontario textbooks at the war's end, although they might reappear in those books published after 1885 as bloodthirsty, albeit conquered, "savages" in the Northwest Rebellion. As a study of textbooks used in British Columbia's schools up to the 1960s shows, overall they displayed either repugnance

1 Charles G.D. Roberts, *History of Canada for High Schools and Academies* (Toronto: Morang, 1905), 253.

towards Aboriginal people – depicting them as irrational, bloodthirsty savages – or portrayed them as infantile and in need of paternal guidance. These judgments were conveyed by descriptions of explorers such as Jacques Cartier dispensing trinkets to child-like "Indians" or discussions of the Metis that attributed their participation in the events of 1869–70 and 1885 to their ignorance of the Canadian government's good intentions towards them.

Except for Laura Secord, often the only woman mentioned in these books – in some cases she was joined by Madeleine de Verchères, Jeanne Mance, Catherine Parr Traill, and Susanna Moodie – overall, Canadian women had little or no role to play in the nation's past. Workers did not fare much better: of twenty-nine textbooks published between 1886 and 1979, only a few referred to them. At times, textbooks might introduce workers and some degree of social history with, for example, discussions of society in New France, Loyalists and pioneers, Prairie settlement, the 1919 Winnipeg General Strike, or the Depression. However, conflicts between labour, the state, and capital were rarely discussed and students would have received little sense of the role of unions in fighting for better working conditions. Canadian workers, the textbooks told students, had been peaceful, hardworking, temperate, and, above all, complacent, as they dutifully accepted their place in society. Furthermore, their role in contributing to the nation was seldom acknowledged; it was the general manager of the Canadian Pacific Railway, Cornelius Van Horne, and not workers, who had "built" the CPR.

The 1950s and 1960s witnessed a degree of change in textbooks' content and organization. In Ontario, new curriculum guidelines introduced by the provincial government in 1959 expanded the amount of time given to Canadian history in grades seven, eight, and ten. However, this came with a greater focus on Canada's relationship with the United States. Students at the elementary level were expected to learn about the English colonies of the seventeenth and eighteenth centuries, the American Revolution, the nineteenth-century expansion of the republic, and the U.S. Civil War, as well as the political and military history of New France, the creation of the Canadas, the War of 1812, the Rebellion of 1837, Durham's report and responsible government, railways, Confederation, the Northwest Rebellion, and Laurier's imperial ties. The Maritime provinces and British Columbia received not much more than a passing mention in this narrative. Grade ten students were to learn about twentieth-century events in Canadian history – immigration to the Prairies, the First World War and the Treaty of Versailles, Canada's military role in the First World War – but their attention was to focus on relationships between Canada, Britain, and the United States, with Canada playing a noticeably junior role in this "Atlantic triangle."

Some textbook authors dealt with the new curriculum by attempting to deal with conflict more directly and openly. Edith Deyell's grade-seven text, *Canada: A New Land*, for example, discussed the deportation of the Acadians as a shameful episode in Canada's history. In another work, Deyell also discussed the activism of late-nineteenth- and early-twentieth-century Canadian women, whose experiences of community-building in reform movements such as temperance led a number of them into the fight for suffrage. Others, even before the new guidelines were introduced, introduced sections on so-called "ordinary Canadians" to break up an almost unrelenting focus on political and military history and to integrate social history with other narratives. Donalda Dickie's 1950 book, *The Great Adventure: An Illustrated History of Canada for Young Canadians*, called for a more connected teaching of history, rather than social studies' "bits and patches" approach. "The history of Canada," Dickie argued,

is a thoroughly good story; a "movie" in Technicolour, enacted on a vast stage, by characters lively, intriguing, romantic, wise and

166 Commemorating Canada

foolish, good and bad, but hardly ever dull. It is full of excursions and alarms; hair breadth escapes with life and fortune perched upon a paddle blade; great attempts made boldly, lost or won gaily; important events with at least one development that has played, and is playing an important part in the evolution of the free world of today.[2]

Yet, despite such good intentions, the textbooks of the 1950s and 1960s still demonstrated a strong desire to downplay internal conflicts and power relations and stereotyped those, such as French Canadians, who could not be easily integrated into narratives of progress, prosperity, and consensus that focused on English-speaking Canada. George W. Brown's *Building the Canadian Nation* and J.W. Chafe and Arthur R.M. Lower's *Canada, a Nation and How It Came to Be* demonstrate how pervasive and long-lasting these stereotypes were. Brown's *Building the Canadian Nation* was a grade-ten text first published in 1942 and, with some additions and rewordings, it was used in Ontario from 1945 to 1959 and authorized by the Departments of Education in Newfoundland, Nova Scotia, New Brunswick, Manitoba, and Alberta, and by Protestant school boards in Quebec, while Chafe and Lower's book was authorized for Ontario schools. Both books portrayed French Canadians as exotic and different; lacking formal education, they tended to be unambitious, cheerful, easy-going, insular, and unchanging habitants and voyageurs. Both books, as well, drew upon nineteenth-century American historian Francis Parkman's work, although neither used Parkman's more positive depictions of French Canadians, nor did they draw upon the available primary sources that spoke of French Canadians' enterprise, women's domestic labour, or the presence of primary schools in New France.

---

2 Donalda Dickie, *The Great Adventure: An Illustrated History of Canada for Young Canadians* (Toronto: J.M. Dent, 1950), vii.

Alongside textbooks, though, the elementary-level readers mentioned earlier in this chapter educated children about the past by focusing on individuals whose lives were meant to provide moral examples and inspiration. The books also were intended to teach literacy, cultural knowledge, and a basis for further historical study. According to their authors, biography "was the best medium through which to approach the study of history. The dry, dull facts of social and political changes are coloured, illuminated, and given an interest through the intimate association with great men and women of the past."[3] These great men and women, though, might be seen as exemplifying key national characteristics, whether it was Father Jean de Brébeuf's self-sacrifice, Isaac Brock's heroism, Robert Baldwin's persistence, Egerton Ryerson's zeal for education, or John A. Macdonald and Wilfrid Laurier's aspirations for the country. Like historical landmarks and sites, then, these individuals were seen as the repositories of historical and national meanings, representative of Canada at its various stages of development. However, unlike the textbooks, readers might include more portraits of women as historical actors. While the Ryerson Canadian History Readers Series or Macmillan's Canadian Men of Action paid far more attention to men, other readers provided both girls and boys with more detailed versions of women's lives – Françoise-Marie Jacquelin, Madame de la Tour, and Marie Rollet, the first French female settler – that textbooks discussed only briefly. Although the "heyday" of the readers appears to have been the interwar years, they survive today as children's history books, both factual and fictional, with the notable difference that the individuals they highlight come from a wider swathe of Canadian society and include immigrants, First Nations, and African-Americans.

---

3 W.J. Karr, *Explorers, Soldiers, and Statesmen: The History of Canada Through Biography* (Toronto: J.M. Dent, 1929), ix.

Like the erection of monuments or staging of pageants, the study of history in the schools was not without controversy and its critics. Even though many might agree that teaching history was important in shaping future citizens, that did not mean unanimity on history's meaning for citizenship. For some, being a good citizen might mean a more critical analysis of one's country and its past than seeing its history as a story to be celebrated. Writing in *Western School Journal* in 1919, Mildred B. McCallum, the editor of the women's page for *The Grain Grower's Guide*, complained that history was the most "mistaught subject" in the curriculum, as it consisted of nothing more than a chronological recitation of facts that lacked context and analysis and thus could not prepare students for citizenship. Groups such as the Women's International League for Peace and Freedom (WILPF), the United Farmers, and feminist organizations included teachers who might well challenge the status quo and, in the words of today's curriculum experts, "teach against" the curriculum. Of course, criticism of Canada's past was not always welcomed by provincial ministries of education. In January 1920, the British Columbia Department of Education removed G.L. Grant's *History of Canada* from its list of authorized textbooks. Grant, a historian and war hero, had depicted nineteenth-century Metis resistance too sympathetically, the province felt. What was more, his discussion of the First World War was not critical enough of Germany and did not celebrate Britain's participation and effort as much as the department thought fit. The department's action left British Columbia's history teachers without a textbook for that year; instead of teaching history, they focused on civics.

Critics of history education also targeted the way in which the subject was taught for its dullness. A 1933 survey of Canadian history textbooks, prepared by the Canadian branch of WILPF, did not find them excessively nationalist or militaristic but complained that a potentially fascinating subject had been made boring and tedious. Such criticisms persisted into the post–Second World War period; a national survey report on provincial history education condemned it as having been "'factualized' to the point of boredom. All of this resulted in a "'desiccated form of treatment quite sufficient to remove from the Canadian story any kind of glamour or interest which it may have possessed.'"[4]

Moreover, just as monuments and historic sites might be the recipients of more abstract than actual support from levels of government, the teaching of Canadian history experienced similar treatment. For much of the first half of the twentieth century, teachers across the country often lacked the background and training in the subject when they first entered the classroom, let alone the time to keep abreast of new research, to do much more than teach the textbook's standard narratives. Such problems were even more evident in many parts of rural Canada, where school boards lacked the resources – not to mention the inclination – to hire the kinds of subject specialists that might be found in larger, urban schools with specific departments and department heads. A history teacher such as Napanee's Celia File, who earned an MA in History at Queen's University in 1930 for her thesis on Mary Brant and went on to teach in small towns in southwestern Ontario, was rare. To be sure, teachers' publications of the interwar decades demonstrate that history teachers themselves did not always agree that the standard curriculum and textbook approach were best. Their writings demonstrate a desire to teach history through interpretation of sources, to impress on students the need to understand context and complexity, to give their students a range of good written resources and to have them conduct their own research, not just read textbooks, to make the subject relevant, and to expose their

---

4 Ken Osborne, "'Our History Syllabus Has Us Gasping': History in Canadian Schools – Past, Present, and Future," *Canadian Historical Review* 81, no. 3 (September 2000): 415.

students to historical sites, museums, oral histories, and material culture – in short, to deploy practices and achieve goals similar to those of today's high school history teachers and university professors. In Manitoba's schools, for example, by the 1910s some teachers were starting to use art, drama, and literature to supplement their textbooks (Longfellow's *Evangeline* was a popular choice). They also began to use other forms of pedagogy, such as mock trials, elections, and parliaments; in Winnipeg's Model School (a teacher-training institution), history teachers began to bring in group discussions, supplementary reference materials, and oral histories. Manitoba also was notable for the number of politically active history teachers in the province, ones involved in left-wing causes who believed that history teaching should promote a more critical awareness of the country's past, present, and future.

Yet teachers at the high school level were constrained by their students' need to pass standardized province-wide examinations; their ideals for history teaching conflicted with provincial departments of education demands for material that could be memorized, organized, and presented in uniform ways. History teachers' dissatisfaction with the situation led some of them to advocate for a shift to more progressive, child-centred approaches and an interest in the social sciences, which appeared to promise more analytical and intellectually challenging forms of learning. Except for Alberta from 1935 to 1945, where progressive ideas of citizenship shaped the school curriculum in attempts to build a better society, little concrete movement in that direction occurred during the interwar decades. Such approaches became more compelling in the 1960s and 1970s.

Moreover, the types of "national" histories that, as we have seen, were attempted in other forms of public history were equally, perhaps even more, difficult to achieve in Canadian classrooms. For one, education was – and is – a provincial matter. Just as the Diamond Jubilee of Confederation celebrations differed depending on the region in which they were held, so too did narratives of Canada's past differ according to the location of the school in which they were taught. That did not stop politicians from trying to create a unified narrative, though. As history teaching began to appear in schools across the country (while simultaneously monuments, pageants, historical societies, and historic sites also made an appearance on the Dominion's commemorative landscape), the minister of education for Ontario, George Ross, called for a national history with "broad features common to the whole of this Dominion with which we can indoctrinate our pupils, so that when a child takes up the history of Canada, he feels that ... he is taking up the history of a great country."[5] The Dominion Education Association responded to Ross's plea by sponsoring a competition for a national history textbook, won by W.H.P. Clement's *The History of the Dominion of Canada.* Other provincial Ministries of Education, though, were not persuaded by Ross's nationalist rhetoric (or at least did not wish to cede control), and only half of the provinces adopted it. To be sure, the histories narrated in textbooks used across the country adopted a nationalist perspective, particularly after the First World War. By the end of the century, in a case of history – or, in this case, history educators – repeating itself, calls for "national history standards" were made in the 1990s and early 2000s by groups such as the Ontario History and Social Sciences Teachers' Association, calls that were rejected or ignored by those involved in history education in other jurisdictions. The Dominion Institute, an organization formed in 1997 to promote (in their words) a common memory and civic identity in Canada, was also one of the most vocal and visible groups that called for a common history that emphasized nation-building and political

_____

5 Ibid., 404.

events. The Institute's activities have also focused largely on English-Canadian history.

Yet just as other attempts to form seamless or uniform national public histories foundered when their narrators attempted to impose them on Quebec, so too did attempts to achieve the teaching of a "national" history run aground in that province. It is perhaps not surprising that the overarching themes of Canadian history taught for much of this period, ones that relied on the imperial tie, Canada's "origins" as a British colony, and the progress of English-speaking Canada, would have little or no appeal in Quebec. In Quebec texts, the dominant narrative was based on the work of Lionel Groulx: that of the survival of a French Catholic society, told as an inspirational moral tale that highlighted courage and tenacity in the face of (predominantly) exterior threats and hostility. Students learned little about English Canada although, in the interest of fairness, the latter's texts said very little about New France, Lower Canada, or Quebec that was not patronizing, condescending, or considered French Canada to be a "problem." Although Quebec historian Arthur Maheux worried in the 1930s that his province's textbooks taught hatred of English-speaking Canada, his contemporary André Larendeau thought, after reviewing them, that they were more likely to teach children to be bored with the study of history. In a 1990s interview, political leader Lucien Bouchard remarked that the textbooks used by his teachers in the 1950s simply ignored the rest of the country and focused instead on Quebec and Europe.

These critiques of history curriculum and teaching became more public and more charged in the 1960s and 1970s. Some of the intensity came from the rise of social studies and more interdisciplinary forms of study which, while popular amongst certain educators in the 1930s, did not have much of an impact on the actual practices of teaching until the 1960s and beyond. To be sure, there had been criticisms of the texts' political biases much earlier in the century, ones that were joined by individual voices. Starting in the 1930s, the Mohawk teacher and magistrate Oliver Milton Martin (a descendant of the Mohawk collector and doctor Oronhyatekha), who lived and worked in Toronto, voiced vociferous and pointed critiques of textbooks' portrayals of Aboriginal people. In the 1950s, Martin's objections were followed by those of fellow Mohawk and Ontario writer and performer Ethel Brant Monture, who objected to the books' focus on warfare.

However, the rise of a number of radical movements in the 1960s, coupled with new approaches to the writing of history within the academy, meant that the schools' history curricula came under far greater and far more sustained critique. In 1964, the Indian and Metis conference sponsored a report that found textbook representations of their communities to be of either ignorant and simple-minded subhumans or fierce and predatory savages. According to the 1968 *What Culture? What Heritage?* by A.B. Hodgetts, Canadian history as told to history students was not much more than a "bland, consensus story, told without the controversy that is an inherent part of history."[6] It also did little, argued Hodgetts, to counter the "two solitudes" approach towards relations between French and English Canada. A content analysis of social studies textbooks, published by researchers Garnet McDiarmid and David Pratt for the Ontario Institute for Studies in Education in 1971, argued that schools were "teaching prejudice" in the curriculum's treatment of women, Native people, ethnic and racial minorities, and workers.

As 1970s files from Ontario's Ministry of Education suggest, such concerns were not limited to educators. Parents and, in one case, a grandparent wrote in to voice their unhappiness with gender and racial stereotyping. As well,

---

6 A.B. Hodgetts, *What Culture? What Heritage?* (Toronto: Ontario Institute for Studies in Education, 1968), 24.

representatives of organizations weighed in with their concerns. In October 1972, William Mahoney, the national director of the United Steelworkers of America, told the then-minister of education Thomas Wells that labour needed to be included in any attempt to eliminate bias in the schools' teaching of history. Using "Teaching Prejudice," Mahoney pointed to the absence of labour and working-class history from the curriculum, unless the subject was violent upheaval (the Winnipeg General Strike, for example); moreover, students were taught very little about the labour movement's present-day significance. Wells replied that he was aware of the problem and had just met with the Ontario Federation of Labour to discuss solutions. Two years later, N. Keith Lickers, the director of the Woodland Indian Cultural and Educational Centre on the Six Nations reserve, offered his organization's services to the Canadian Book Publishers' Council as a way of countering errors of fact concerning First Nations. The Centre, Lickers told Eileen McAlear, the council's representative, could bring in people who were qualified to edit the subject matter. In 1974, the Manitoba Indian Brotherhood, in their report *The Shocking Truth About Indians in Textbooks,* argued that Indigenous people were treated primarily as impediments to be removed; similar objections were voiced in a report written by Nova Scotia's Human Rights Commission. To these Canadians, history clearly mattered.

Some, though, believed the answer was to shift away from teaching history as a separate discipline. A number of provinces moved from offering history itself as a subject to teaching it through area studies, such as "Atlantic Canadian studies," studies of Western Canada that grouped the Prairie provinces with British Columbia, and Canadian Studies, approaches that had been heavily influenced by American developments in social studies' teaching. In search of a solution to what seemed to him as an intractable problem, Hodgetts shifted to interdisciplinary work and created the Canadian Studies Foundation, which had a strong social-science focus. However, in recent decades, new developments in history pedagogy, both within Canada and internationally, have made the case for teaching history as a separate and distinct subject in ways that, far from inculcating rote memorization, teach students to engage in an active interpretation of and engagement with the past. Some history educators argue that history and citizenship should continue to be linked, albeit in a way that urges students to take a critical and questioning stance towards the nation-state. Others, though, believe that history should be taught as a disciplined inquiry because of its own intrinsic worth and the intellectual excitement that dealing with different interpretations of the past generates.

Curriculum, policy guidelines, and textbook contents are, of course, important aspects of the history of history teaching. Yet, like people's responses to monuments or other commemorative spectacles, it is far more difficult and, for some periods, impossible to determine not just "what was taught" in history classrooms but also how students received and remembered their lessons. For the more recent past, a national survey of Canadians about their sense of history and collective memory has found that 53 per cent of their respondents had found Canadian history interesting; of that group, half mentioned particular teachers, most commonly at the high school level. Such responses make an interesting comparison with the United States, where a similar survey conducted in the 1990s singled out history teaching in the schools as doing more to suppress their interest in the subject.

Nevertheless, although tracking audiences can be a complicated effort, it is possible to make generalizations about the men and women who wrote the majority of textbooks in English Canada. Like those who organized commemorative events or were influential in creating historic sites, they tended to be middle class, often from southern and central Ontario, and university graduates who had taught history at either the secondary or university level. A few also worked for Departments of Education; Deyell, for instance, taught in Ottawa and had been a school inspector in Wentworth County. A minority, albeit a significant one, of these authors were women, a situation not unlike that of the historical societies in which some female writers had been active. In the early decades of the twentieth century, women such as Blanche Hume and Emily Weaver tended to write readers, sketches, or textbooks that were used at the elementary level or as supplements to other textbooks. It is tempting, of course, to see their work as an example of women historians' relegation to a subservient position, either lacking or being denied the more respected and authoritative voice of the writer for senior grades. However, while there may be some degree of truth in this analysis, we should not forget that the readers and elementary-level books may have had an initial and more lasting effect on children's imaginations than the high school textbook, particularly from the 1880s to the 1920s, when the ·majority of Canadians left school at fourteen. Books such as Hume's *Laura Secord*, published in 1928 by Ryerson Press as part of its Canadian History Readers Series and authorized by both the Ontario Department of Education and the Imperial Order Daughters of the Empire, or Weaver's *A Canadian History for Boys and Girls*, published in 1905, may well have left a greater impression on children than W.L. Grant's 1914 *Ontario High School History of Canada* (one wonders if the 1960 work of Luella Creighton, married to historian Donald Creighton, may have had a similar effect).

Women continued to write history textbooks in the postwar decades, in some cases continuing successful work that they had begun in the interwar decades. Donalda Dickie, Ontario-born, Alberta-based historian and an author of books on a number of topics related to education, published *The Great Adventure: An Illustrated History of Canada for Young Canadians* in 1950, a book that sold over 50,000 copies, went through multiple printings in the decade, and won the Governor-General's Award for the best book of juvenile literature published in 1950. Her contemporary,

Manitoba-based teacher Aileen Garland, who trained at the Universities of Toronto and Manitoba, wrote a number of history texts and readers, including *Canada, Then and Now* (1954) and *Canada, Our Country* (1961); both books were published by Toronto's Macmillan. Garland was also a member of the Manitoba Historical Society and contributed articles on the province's history.

Yet until the 1980s, the discipline of Canadian history as practised in the country's universities was dominated by men; it was probably not a coincidence that many of the most widely used high school history texts in the postwar decades were written by male historians based in university history departments. Such was the case with George W. Brown, a University of Michigan PhD who taught Canadian and American history at the University of Toronto, was president of the Canadian Historical Association in 1944, and helped found the *Dictionary of Canadian Biography*. Brown was far from being the only academic historian to help shape students' understanding of their past, though. His contemporary, Arthur Lower, the co-author of *Canada, a Nation and How It Came to Be*, was a Harvard PhD who taught at Queen's University. *Our Canada*, published in 1949, was written by the University of Western Ontario's Arthur G. Dorland, whose academic work focused on the history of Canada's Quakers. In the 1960s and 1970s, other prominent academic historians, such as Ramsay Cook, Kenneth McNaught, Stanley Mealing, John S. Moir, and Robert Craig Brown, wrote texts either for the schools or for use as supplementary material for upper-level high school courses. In 1967, three Quebec historians, Jean Hamelin, Fernand Ouellet, and Marcel Trudel, joined forces with anglophone historian Paul Cornell to produce the text, *Canada: Unité et diversité* (although by then both Trudel and Ouellet were employed at Ontario universities). In English, the book's subtitle was – interestingly enough – *Unity in Diversity*.

Despite the work of these historians, over the course of the twentieth century, a growing rift emerged between those who taught history in the schools and university-based historians. Such a distance was not unique to Canada; in the American context, historian Gary B. Nash has called this the "long walk" by historians from the schools. Nor was it to be found only in formal education; the professionalization of Canadian history in the 1920s and 1930s also meant that historians attempted to put considerable distance between themselves and members of local historical societies, dismissing the latter's work as narrow, antiquarian, and not scholarly. While some prominent historians, such as Creighton and, more recently, Veronica Strong-Boag and Margaret Conrad, have sat on the Historic Sites and Monuments Board, increasingly historians generally tended to work within the structures (some might say strictures) of the academy and their departments, a trend that caused some historians considerable anxiety in the 1990s. (Of course, like any historical process there were a number of exceptions to this pattern; historians may well have been more involved in local, regional, and provincial groups, a "history" that awaits its historian.) The Canadian Historical Association, though, attempted to bring teachers into the organization in the 1920s and 1930s, with proposed initiatives such as a lecture series for teachers, invitations to attend its meetings, discussions with local schools, and, in the early 1950s, the Historical Booklet Series, meant to provide teachers and students with succinct discussions of significant events, processes, and individuals written by recognized experts in the field. Although one of its earliest proposed booklets, a study of Riel, was rejected by the Ontario Department of Education for being too controversial, in 1953, the department bought 1,000 copies of the first booklet, military historian C.P. Stacey's *The Undefended Border.* Nevertheless, despite these and other efforts aimed at integrating local history within the Canadian Historical Association (which might also have drawn in teachers), history teachers found their interests best served within their own professional organizations. In the very recent past, they have also been courted by groups such as the Historica-Dominion Institute (founded in 2009 out of a merger of Historica and the Dominion Institute) and Canada's National History Society, organizations that reflect late-twentieth-century English-speaking Canadians' ongoing fascination with their history.

In many ways, Canadian schoolchildren linked the commemorative work and public memories described in the previous chapters. In the late nineteenth and early twentieth century, the historical narratives that they learned from their texts and readers, with their explorers, politicians, soldiers, and religious leaders, had been written by either those active in historical societies or authors who had been influenced by the work of these groups. As time went on, it is not too far-fetched to suppose that the narratives children learned in school helped shape adults' broad-based public understanding of what constituted the central themes and events of Canada's past. Furthermore, museums and historic sites increasingly were seen both by educators and those who ran them as important places in which children might learn social and cultural history, whether that meant gazing at artefacts housed in glass cases at provincial or local museums, participating in military drills at forts, or churning butter under the guidance of costumed interpreters at Ontario's Black Creek Pioneer Village. Children's historic pageants, whether to mark Empire Day in Ontario or across the country on 1 July 1967, also owed their existence to the early twentieth century's fascination with public and performed displays of the past. To be sure, over the course of the twentieth century, university-based history teaching progressively separated itself from the work of commemorators and the so-called amateur historian. Nevertheless, it's not hard to imagine that at least some undergraduates were drawn to their first university history course after participating in such historical re-enactments and performances, their imaginations sparked by "becoming" historical subjects, as well as by their elementary and high school history lessons.

8

Epilogue

Canadians' interest in the past, it has been argued, has been steadily growing since at least the 1970s, with an increase in those involved in genealogical research, the popularity of best-selling authors of popular history such as Peter C. Newman, Pierre Berton, and Jacques Lacoursière, and, in the past thirty years, the fascination of Canadian novelists and playwrights – Margaret Atwood, Guy Vanderhaeghe, Arlette Cousture, David French, Michel Marc Bouchard, and Ann Marie Macdonald, to name just a few – with historical fiction and drama. To this list we can add series such as CBC-TV-Radio Canada's *Canada: A People's History*, the formation of organizations such as the Canada's National History Society, the Dominion Institute and the Historica Foundation (the latter two of which have since merged). As well, there is also the ongoing popularity of the popular English-Canadian history magazine, *The Beaver* (renamed *Canada's History* in 2010), and the Québécois magazine, *Cap-aux-Diamants*.

Yet, while there is a degree of truth in this argument, in that there are a wide range of historical genres, fora, and institutions available to Canadians, stating that this is somehow unprecedented or represents a new departure from past commemorative practices overstates matters. Canadians have not been uninterested or unconcerned with their histories, whether that concern was expressed in historical novels, historical texts, raising monuments, or commemorating historic sites and landscapes. Even genealogy, in its nineteenth-century manifestation, more visible as a phenomenon limited to the elite or to those with aspirations to elite status, was an important methodology among nineteenth- and twentieth-century Acadians and northwestern Saskatchewan's Metis. While Canada's wartime participation has received increased public attention since the 1990s, putting up monuments to battles fought both here and overseas is a process that, as we have seen, has its own history. Moreover, although it can be difficult to quantify the ways in which community and family histories were transmitted orally in the more distant past, these practices have been integral to Aboriginal communities' sense of self. Judging from research in working-class and immigration history, they also have a long "history" in those communities as well. Furthermore, oral reminiscences made their appearances in middle-class historical societies' reports for the late nineteenth century; oral history is not a phenomenon confined to those communities excluded from the written record.

Perhaps what has changed in the last few decades is the greater range of communities and individuals interested in history who now have greater political, cultural, and social resources in which to express that interest and, hence, a wider range of venues that are more highly visible to other groups and the media. Their concern about the past can be expressed in a number of ways. In 1992, Irish-Canadians, whose nineteenth-century history incorporated the Famine migration of 1847 as a definitive moment (as opposed to being part of a longer history of migration), engaged in heated debates over the creation of Grosse Ile, the site of a major quarantine station, as a national historic site. They believed that Parks Canada's proposal would result in a more generic monument to Canadian migration (Parks Canada ended up featuring the Irish at the site). This was not the first time, though, that Irish-Catholics had sought to have their ancestors' Famine experiences memorialized. The Ship Fever Monument in Montreal's Pointe Sainte-Charles, first erected in 1859, has been an important site for the city's Irish-Catholic community to affirm both religious and national identity. More recently, in 2007, members of the Irish-Canadian community erected a memorial, Ireland Park, to those who died upon their arrival in Toronto. Others have called upon levels of government to redress past injustices, as in the case of the internments of Italians, Ukrainians, and Japanese-Canadians during the world wars, or Chinese-Canadians who have lobbied for restitution for the head taxes and racist exclusion imposed on them by the Dominion government. The history of the Holocaust has become central to much elementary and high school history teaching across Canada, both as part of the history of the spread of fascism and antisemitism in early-twentieth-century Europe and that of the Second World War and as a means of teaching students, particularly in the elementary grades, about the dangers of intolerance and racism. Interviews with Holocaust survivors and texts – in particular, *The Diary of Anne Frank* – have played a significant role in this pedagogy. In 2004, the Canadian government declared 15 April to be Canadian Holocaust Remembrance Day, which ties Canadian antisemitism to the Nazi genocide. Recently, the Canadian Museum of Immigration, housed at Halifax's Pier 21, opened a memorial, the Wheel of Conscience, to those European Jews refused entry by the federal government in the 1930s.

First Nations communities across Canada weave a sense of their history, whether that of pre-contact times or of relations with settler society and the Canadian government, into a myriad of cultural, spiritual, socio-economic, and political questions and issues. These range from land treaties, resource rights, and residential schools to assertions of Indigenous cultural practices and languages. Although First Nations' consciousness of their past is hardly new, this history has achieved greater visibility, thanks in part to the 1996 *Report of the Royal Commission on Aboriginal Peoples* and revelations about the abuses suffered by Aboriginal students in residential schools. At times, the site of the latter may be reclaimed by Aboriginal communities for their own purposes, as in the Six Nations' use of the former Mohawk Institute for the Woodland Cultural Centre, which houses an important archival collection, library, and museum. For their part, African-Canadian communities, long denied a historical presence in Canada's public history by racist means of exclusion that declared them either invisible or insignificant, have crafted their own narratives that establish their past in this country through museums, works of popular history, and forms of artistic expression that include fiction, drama, poetry, and song.

Canadian women, who have had a fairly lengthy history as their own and as their community's, province's, and nation's historians, have been active in the creation of monuments and historic sites dedicated to first-wave feminists (the Famous Five) and social reformers (the Women's Institutes). They have also created archives, such as the Canadian Women's Movement Archives, which began its life as an independent institution in Toronto and is now part of the University of Ottawa's special collections. Canadian feminists also mark a number of events: Women's History Month, held in October; International Women's Day on 8 March; and the commemoration of the Montreal Massacre on 6 December. Moreover, while the range of women remembered by government and voluntary organizations and individuals is still much smaller than that of their male counterparts, it has expanded to include Aboriginal and African-Canadian women, such as Shawnadithit, Thanadelthur, Mary Anne Shadd Carey, and Viola Desmond.

Long "hidden from history" because of homophobia, gay and lesbian communities across Canada have worked to craft their own historical narratives, through archival collections of text and material culture, oral histories, and a variety of performances, the latter ranging from Pride Day Parades to theatre and film. While workers and the left in Canada are still under-represented in public history, the creation of institutions such as Hamilton's Workers' Arts and Heritage Centre, the monuments to the Mackenzie-Papineau Battalion, and the National Day of Mourning, 28 April, for workers killed on the job, maintain a collective memory that both celebrates the activism of Canada's working classes and the left, here and abroad, and reminds Canadians of the unequal relations within capitalism.

Future historians of commemoration and collective memory thus will have a rich array of sources from which they can explore both continuity and change in the creation of historical memories. Whether such narratives will differ dramatically in tone from those produced in the nineteenth and twentieth centuries is, of course, a matter of debate. Communities that now insist on their inclusion in the commemorative landscape can also fall prey to the allure of simplistic and celebratory histories that gloss over internal conflicts, ignore complexities, or downplay less-appealing aspects of their pasts. Historians of Italian-Canadian internment, for example, point to the very real presence of fascists within the Italian community of the 1930s and 1940s, while those who wish to remember first-wave feminists need to reckon with some of these women's class and racial prejudices and support for causes such as eugenics.

Canadians' need to commemorate and remember in multiple venues and for multiple reasons tells us much about the centrality of the past to our identities and the many ways in which it matters, not just to governments and elites but to a wide range of groups within Canadian society. Examining the "history of history-making" in our past can help us think more profoundly about the ways in which we use "history," both in the present and future. We need to ask the same questions of twenty-first-century commemorators as we do of their nineteenth- and twentieth-century predecessors. Why, when, where, and for whom is the past meaningful? What are the ramifications for Canadians, both participants and spectators, when certain pasts are remembered and others are forgotten?

Bibliography

Chapter One

Berger, Carl. *The Writing of Canadian History: Aspects of English-Canadian Historical Writing since 1900.* 2nd ed. Toronto: University of Toronto Press, 1987.

Caron, Caroline-Isabelle. "Patrimoine, généalogie et identité: La valorisation de la mémoire familiale au Québec et en Acadie au XXᵉ siècle." *Enfances, Familles, Générations* 7 (Fall 2007): 1–12, http://www.erudit.org/revue/efg/2007/v/n7/index.html

Confino, Alon. "Collective Memory and Cultural History: Problems of Method." *American Historical Review* 102, no. 5 (December 1997): 1386–403.

Cubitt, Geoffrey. *History and Memory.* Manchester: Manchester University Press, 2007.

Fentress, James, and Chris Wickham. *Social Memory.* London: Blackwell, 1992.

Hobsbawm, Eric, and Terence Ranger, eds. *The Invention of Tradition.* Cambridge: Cambridge University Press, 1983.

Kammen, Michael. *Mystic Chords of Memory: The Transformation of Tradition in American Culture.* New York: Vintage Books, 1993.

Lowenthal, David. *The Heritage Crusade and the Spoils of History.* London: Penguin Books, 1996.

– *The Past Is a Foreign Country.* Cambridge: Cambridge University Press, 1985.

Macdougall, Brenda. "Wahkootowin: Family and Cultural Identity in Northwestern Saskatchewan Metis Communities." *Canadian Historical Review* 87, no. 3 (September 2006): 431–62.

McAllister, Kirsten Emiko. "Archive and Myth: The Changing Memoryscape of Japanese Canadian Internment Camps." In *Placing Memory and Remembering Place in Canada,* edited by James Opp and John C. Walsh, 215–46. Vancouver: University of British Columbia Press, 2010.

Neatby, Nicole, and Peter Hodgins, eds. *Settling and Unsettling Memories: Essays in Canadian Public History.* Toronto: University of Toronto Press, 2012.

Nora, Pierre, and Lawrence D. Kritzman, eds. *Realms of Memory: Rethinking the French Past.* Translated by Arthur Goldhammer. 3 vols. New York: Columbia University Press, 1996–98.

Phillips, Mark Salber, and Gordon Schochet, eds. *Questions of Tradition.* Toronto: University of Toronto Press, 2004.

Samuel, Raphael. *Theatres of Memory.* Vol. 1, *Past and Present in Contemporary Culture.* London: Verso, 1994.

Shaw, Christopher, and Malcolm Chase, eds. *The Imagined Past: History and Nostalgia.* Manchester: Manchester University Press, 1989.

Wright, Donald. *The Professionalization of History in English Canada.* Toronto: University of Toronto Press, 2005.

Wright, Patrick. *On Living in an Old Country: The National Past in Contemporary Britain.* London: Verso, 1985.

Chapter Two

Dictionary of Canadian Biography, accessible online at http://www. biographi.ca/en/index.php. University of Toronto/Université Laval: 2003–2015.

Beasley, David R. "Richardson, John," 1851–1860 *(Volume VIII).*

Chassé, Béatrice. "Labrie, Jacques," 1821–1835 *(Volume VI).*

Morgan, Cecilia. "Carnochan, Janet," 1921–1930 *(Volume XV).*

Savard, Pierre, and Paul Wyczynski. "Garneau, François-Xavier," 1861–1870 *(Volume IX).*

Stockdale, J.C. "Mullins, Rosanna Eleanora (Leprohon)," 1871–1880 *(Volume X).*

Trofimenkoff, Susan Mann. "Foster, Eliza Lanesford (Cushing)," 1881–1890 *(Volume XI)*.

Béland, Mario. *Paintings in Quebec 1820–1850: New Views, New Perspectives*. Quebec: Musée du Québec, 1992.

Bernatchez, Ginette. "La Société littéraire et historique de Québec (The Literary and Historical Society of Quebec), 1824–1890." *Revue d'histoire de l'Amérique française* 35, no. 2 (1981): 179–92.

Clarke, George Elliott. "'This Is No Hearsay': Reading the Canadian Slave Narratives." *Papers of the Bibliographical Society of Canada* 43, no. 1 (Spring 2005): 7–26.

Cottrell, Michael. "St Patrick's Day Parades in Nineteenth-Century Toronto: A Study of Immigrant Adjustment and Elite Control." In *A Nation of Immigrants: Women, Workers, and Communities in Canadian History, 1840s–1960s*, edited by Franca Iacovetta, Paula Draper, and Robert Ventresca, 35–54. Toronto: University of Toronto Press, 1998.

Drew, Benjamin. *The Narratives of Fugitive Slaves in Canada*. Toronto: Coles, 1981. First published in Boston in 1856 by John P. Jewett and Company.

Frost, Karolyn Smardz, ed. *Ontario's African-Canadian Heritage: Collected Writings by Fred Landon, 1918–1967*. Toronto: Natural Heritage Books, 2009.

Gagnon, Hervé. "Divertissement et patriotisme: La genèse des musées d'histoire à Montréal au XIXe siècle." *Revue d'histoire de l'Amérique française* 48, no. 3 (1995): 317–49.

Gasbarrone, Lisa M. "Narrative, Memory, and Identity in François-Xavier Garneau's *Histoire du Canada*." *Quebec Studies* 34 (Fall–Winter 2002): 31–46.

Gordon, Alan. *The Hero and the Historians: Historiography and the Uses of Jacques Cartier*. Vancouver: University of British Columbia Press, 2010.

Groulx, Patrice. *Pièges de la mémoire: Dollard des Ormeaux, les Amérindiens et nous*. Hull, QC: Vents d'Ouest, 1998.

Harvey, Kathryn. "Location, Location, Location: David Ross McCord and the Makings of Canadian History." *Journal of the Canadian Historical Association/Revue de la Société historique du Canada* 19, no. 1 (2008): 57–82.

Heron, Craig, and Steve Penfold. "The Craftsman's Spectacle: Labour Day Parades in Canada, The Early Years." *Histoire sociale/ Social History* 29, no. 58 (November 1996): 357–90.

Houston, Cecil J., and William J. Smyth. *The Sash Canada Wore: A Historical Geography of the Orange Order in Canada.* Toronto: University of Toronto Press, 1980.

Killan, Gerald. *David Boyle: From Artisan to Archaeologist.* Toronto: University of Toronto Press, 1983.

Létourneau, Jocelyn. *"Je me souviens."* In *The Oxford Companion to Canadian History,* edited by Gerald Hallowell, 329–30. Toronto: Oxford University Press, 2004.

Martin, Denis. *Portraits des Héros de la Nouvelle-France. Images d'un culte historique.* Quebec: Éditions Hurtubise, 1988.

Mathieu, Jacques, and Jacques Lacoursière. *Les mémoires québécoises.* Sainte-Foy, QC: Presses de l'Université Laval, 1991.

McTavish, Lianne. "Learning to See in New Brunswick, 1862–1929." *Canadian Historical Review* 87, no. 4 (December 2006): 553–81.

Nicks, Trudy. "Dr. Oronhyatekha's History Lessons: Reading Museum Collection as Texts." In *Reading Beyond Words: Contexts for Native History,* edited by Jennifer S.H. Brown and Elizabeth Vibert, 482–508. Peterborough, ON: Broadview Press, 1996.

Peyer, Bernd C. *The Tutor'd Mind: Indian Missionary-Writers in Antebellum America.* Amherst: University of Massachusetts Press, 1997.

Radforth, Ian. *Royal Spectacle: The 1860 Visit of the Prince of Wales to Canada and the United States.* Toronto: University of Toronto Press, 2004.

Reimer, Chad. *Writing British Columbia History, 1784–1958.* Vancouver: University of British Columbia Press, 2009.

Richter, Daniel K. *Ordeal of the Longhouse: The Peoples of the Iroquois League in the Era of European Colonization.* Chapel Hill: University of North Carolina Press, 1992.

Robichaud, Deborah. "Evangeline, a Tale of Acadie." In *History of the Book in Canada.* Vol. 2, 1840–1918, edited by Yvan Lamonde, Patricia Lockhart Fleming, and Fiona A. Black, 59–62. Toronto: University of Toronto Press, 2005.

Schenck, Theresa. "William W. Warren's *History of the Ojibway People*: Tradition, History, and Context." In *Reading Beyond Words: Contexts for Native History*, edited by Jennifer S.H. Brown and Elizabeth Vibert. Peterborough, ON: Broadview Press, 1996.

Smith, Donald. *Sacred Feathers: The Reverend Peter Jones (Kahkewaquonaby) and the Mississauga Indians*. Toronto: University of Toronto Press, 1987.

Taylor, Brook M. *Promoters, Patriots, and Partisans: Historiography in Nineteenth-Century English Canada*. Toronto: University of Toronto Press, 1989.

Teather, Lynne. *The Royal Ontario Museum: A Prehistory, 1830–1914*. Concord, ON: Canada University Press, 2005.

Walden, Keith. *Becoming Modern in Toronto: The Industrial Exhibition and the Shaping of a Late Victorian Culture*. Toronto: University of Toronto Press, 1997.

Williams, Dorothy W. "Print and Black Canadian Culture." In *History of the Book in Canada*. Vol. 2, 1840–1918, edited by Yvan Lamonde, Patricia Lockhart Fleming, and Fiona A. Black, 40–3. Toronto: University of Toronto Press, 2005.

Chapter Three

Caron, Caroline-Isabelle. "Se souvenir de l'Acadie d'antan: Représentations du passé historique dans le cadre de célébrations commémoratives locales en Nouvelle-Écosse au milieu du 20ᵉ siècle." *Acadiensis* 36, no. 1 (Spring 2007): 55–71.

Coates, Colin M., and Cecilia Morgan. *Heroines and History: Representations of Madeleine de Verchères and Laura Secord*. Toronto: University of Toronto Press, 2002.

Cupido, Robert. "Appropriating the Past: Pageants, Politics, and the Diamond Jubilee of Confederation." *Journal of the Canadian Historical Association/Revue de la Société historique du Canada* 9, no. 1 (1998): 155–86.

Furniss, Elizabeth. "Pioneers, Progress, and the Myth of the Frontier: The Landscape of Public History in Rural British Columbia." *BC Studies* 115/116 (Fall 1997): 7–44.

Glassberg, David. *American Historical Pageantry: The Use of Tradition in the Early Twentieth Century.* Chapel Hill: University of North Carolina Press, 1990.

Gordon, Alan. *The Hero and the Historians: Historiography and the Uses of Jacques Cartier.* Vancouver: University of British Columbia Press, 2010.

– *Making Public Pasts: The Contested Terrain of Montreal's Public Memory, 1891–1930.* Montreal: McGill-Queen's University Press, 2001.

Groulx, Patrice. *Pièges de la mémoire: Dollard des Ormeaux, les Amérindiens et nous.* Hull, QC: Vents d'Ouest, 1998.

Henry, Wade A. "Imagining the Great White Mother and the Great King: Aboriginal Tradition and Royal Representation at the 'Great Pow-wow' of 1901." *Journal of the Canadian Historical Association/Revue de la Société historique du Canada* 11, no. 1 (2000): 87–108.

Killan, Gerald. *Preserving Ontario's Heritage: A History of the Ontario Historical Society.* Ottawa: Ontario Historical Society, 1976.

Knowles, Norman. *Inventing the Loyalists: The Ontario Loyalist Tradition and the Creation of Usable Pasts.* Toronto: University of Toronto Press, 1997.

Lears, T.J. Jackson. *No Place of Grace: Antimodernism and the Transformation of American Culture, 1880–1920.* Chicago: University of Chicago Press, 1983.

Marquis, Greg. "Celebrating Champlain in the Loyalist City: Saint John, 1904–10." *Acadiensis* 33, no. 2 (Spring 2004): 27–43.

– "Commemorating the Loyalists in the Loyalist City: Saint John, New Brunswick, 1833–1914." *Urban History Review* 33, no. 1 (Fall 2004): 24–33.

Nelles, H.V. *The Art of Nation-Building: Spectacle and Pageantry at Quebec's Tercentenary.* Toronto: University of Toronto Press, 1999.

Norman, Alison. "'A Highly Favoured People': The Planter Narrative and the 1928 Grand Historic Pageant of Kentville, Nova Scotia." *Acadiensis* 38, no. 2 (Summer–Autumn 2009): 116–40.

Osborne, Brian S. "Constructing Landscapes of Power: The George Etienne Cartier Monument, Montreal." *Journal of Historical Geography* 24, no. 4 (1998): 431–58.

Pass, Forrest D. "'The Wondrous Story and Traditions of the Country': The Native Sons of British Columbia and the Role of Myth in the Formation of an Urban Middle Class." *BC Studies* 151 (Autumn 2006): 3–39.

Pope, Peter E. *The Many Landfalls of John Cabot.* Toronto: University of Toronto Press, 1997.

Rudin, Ronald. *Founding Fathers: The Celebration of Champlain and Laval in the Streets of Quebec, 1878–1908.* Toronto: University of Toronto Press, 2003.

Savage, Kirk. *Standing Soldiers, Kneeling Slaves: Race, War, and Monument in Nineteenth-Century America.* New Haven, CT: Princeton University Press, 1997.

Shipley, Robert. *To Mark Our Place: A History of Canadian War Memorials.* Toronto: NC Press, 1987.

Smzr, Jirí. "Cabot 400: The 1897 St. John's Celebration." *Newfoundland Studies* 12, no. 1 (1996): 16–31.

Swyripa, Frances. *Storied Landscapes: Ethno-Religious Identity and the Canadian Prairies.* Winnipeg: University of Manitoba Press, 2010.

Tickner, Lisa. *The Spectacle of Women: Imagery of the Suffrage Campaign 1907–1914.* Chicago: University of Chicago Press, 1988.

Walsh, John C. "Performing Public Memory and Re-Placing Home in the Ottawa Valley, 1900–1958." In *Placing Memory and Remembering Place in Canada,* edited by James Opp and John C. Walsh, 25–56. Vancouver: University of British Columbia Press, 2010.

Williams, Paul. "Erecting 'an Instructive Object': The Case of the Halifax Memorial Tower." *Acadiensis* 36, no. 2 (Spring 2007): 91–112.

Chapter Four

Bothwell, Robert, Randall Hansen, and Margaret MacMillan. "Controversy, Commemoration, and Capitulation: The Canadian War Museum and Bomber Command." *Queen's Quarterly* 115, no. 3 (Fall 2008): 367–87.

Bower, Shannon. "'Practical Results': The Riel Statue Controversy at the Manitoba Legislative Building." *Manitoba History* 42 (Autumn–Winter 2001–2002): 30–9.

Carr, Graham. "Rules of Engagement: Public History and the Drama of Legitimation." *Canadian Historical Review* 86, no. 2 (June 2005): 317–54.

Carter, Sarah. *Capturing Women: The Manipulation of Cultural Imagery in Canada's Prairie West.* Montreal: McGill-Queen's University Press, 1997.

Dick, Lyle. "Sergeant Masumi Mitsui and the Japanese Canadian War Memorial: Intersections of National, Cultural, and Personal Memory." *Canadian Historical Review* 91, no. 3 (September 2010): 435–63.

Evans, Suzanne. *Mothers of Heroes, Mothers of Martyrs: World War I and the Politics of Grief.* Montreal: McGill-Queen's University Press, 2007.

Harding, Robert J. "Glorious Tragedy: Newfoundland's Cultural Memory of the Attack at Beaumont Hamel, 1916–1925." *Newfoundland and Labrador Studies* 21, no. 1 (2006): 3–40.

Hayes, Geoffrey. "War and Historical Memory." *Acadiensis* 37, no. 2 (Summer–Autumn 2008): 140–7.

Lackenbauer, Whitney P. "War, Memory, and the Newfoundland Regiment at Gallipoli." *Newfoundland Studies* 15, no. 2 (1999): 176–214.

McKay, Ian, and Jamie Swift. *Warrior Nation: Rebranding Canada in an Age of Anxiety.* Toronto: Between the Lines Press, 2012.

McPherson, Kathryn. "Carving Out a Past: The Canadian Nurses' Association War Memorial." *Histoire sociale/Social History* 29, no. 58 (November 1996): 418–29.

Millar, Carman. *Painting the Map Red: Canada and the South African War, 1899–1902.* Montreal: McGill-Queen's University Press, 1997.

Osborne, Brian S. "Corporeal Politics and the Body Politic: The Re-presentation of Louis Riel in Canadian Identity." *International Journal of Heritage Studies* 8, no. 4 (2002): 303–22.

Petrou, Michael. *Renegades: Canadians in the Spanish Civil War.* Vancouver: University of British Columbia Press, 2008.

Pickles, Katie. *Transnational Outrage: The Death and Commemoration of Edith Cavell.* Basingstoke, UK: Palgrave Macmillan, 2007.

Reilly, Sharon. "Robert Kell and the Art of the Winnipeg General Strike." *Labour/Le Travail* 20 (Fall 1987): 182–92.

Richler, Noah. *What We Talk About When We Talk About War.* Fredericton, NB: Goose Lane Editions, 2012.

Shipley, Robert. *To Mark Our Place: A History of Canadian War Memorials.* Toronto: NC Press, 1987.

Vance, Jonathan. *Death So Noble: Memory, Meaning, and the First World War.* Vancouver: University of British Columbia Press, 1997.

Chapter Five

Dodd, Dianne. "Canadian Historic Sites and Plaques: Heroines, Trailblazers, The Famous Five." *CRM: The Journal of Heritage Stewardship* 6, no. 2 (Summer 2009): 29–66.

Duffy, Dennis. "Triangulating the ROM." *Journal of Canadian Studies-Revue d'études canadiennes* 40, no. 1 (Winter 2006): 157–81.

Gordon, Alan. "Heritage and Authenticity: The Case of Ontario's Sainte-Marie-among-the-Hurons." *Canadian Historical Review* 85, no. 3 (September 2004): 507–31.

– "Pioneer Living 1963 Style: Imaginations of Heritage in a Post-war Canadian Suburb." *International Journal of Heritage Studies* 15, no. 6 (2009): 479–93.

Groulx, Patrice. "Benjamin Sulte, père de la commemoration." *Journal of the Canadian Historical Association/Revue de la Société historique du Canada New Series* 12, no. 1 (2001): 49–72.

Hamilton, Michelle A. *Collections and Objections: Aboriginal Material Culture in Southern Ontario.* Montreal: McGill-Queen's University Press, 2010.

Kaye, Frances W. *Hiding the Audience: Viewing Arts and Arts Institutions on the Prairies.* Edmonton: University of Alberta Press, 2003.

Lacasse, Danielle, and Antonio Lechasseur. *The National Archives of Canada 1872–1997.* Ottawa: Canadian Historical Association, 1997.

Litt, Paul. *The Muses, the Masses, and the Massey Commission.* Toronto: University of Toronto Press, 1992.

Marsters, Roger. "'The Battle of Grand Pré': The Historic Sites and Monuments Board of Canada and the Commemoration of Acadian History." *Acadiensis* 36, no. 1 (Autumn 2006): 29–50.

Pannekoek, Fritz. "Canada Historic Sites: Reflections on a Quarter Century, 1980–2005." *The Public Historian* 31, no. 1 (February 2009): 69–88.

Pelletier, Yves. "The Politics of Selection: The Historic Sites and Monuments Board of Canada and the Imperial Commemoration of Canadian History, 1919–1950." *Journal of the Canadian Historical Association/Revue de la Société historique du Canada* 17, no. 1 (2006): 125–50.

Phillips, Ruth. "Re-placing Objects: Historical Practices for the Second Museum Age." *Canadian Historical Review* 86, no. 1 (March 2005): 83–110.

Ricketts, Shannon. "Cultural Selection and National Identity: Establishing Historic Sites in a National Framework, 1920–1939." *The Public Historian* 18, no. 3 (Summer 1996): 23–41.

Taylor, C.J. *Negotiating the Past: The Making of Canada's National Historic Parks and Sites.* Montreal: McGill-Queen's University Press, 1990.

– "Some Early Problems of the Historic Sites and Monuments Board of Canada." *Canadian Historical Review* 64, no. 1 (March 1983): 3–24.

Thomas, Owen. "Cultural Tourism, Commemorative Plaques, and African-Canadian Historiography: Challenging Historical Marginality." *Histoire sociale/Social History* 29, no. 58 (November 1996): 431–9.

Wright, Donald. *The Canadian Historical Association: A History.* Ottawa: Canadian Historical Association, 2003.

Chapter Six

Browne, Dona. *Inventing New England: Regional Tourism in the 19th Century.* Washington, DC: Smithsonian Institution Press, 1995.

Dawson, Michael. *The Mountie from Dime Novel to Disney.* Toronto: Between the Lines Press, 1998.

– *Selling British Columbia: Tourism and Consumer Culture, 1880–1970.* Vancouver: University of British Columbia Press, 2004.

Dubinsky, Karen. *"The Second Greatest Disappointment": Honeymooning and Tourism at Niagara Falls.* Peterborough, ON: Broadview Press, 1999.

Handler, Richard. *Nationalism and the Politics of Culture in Quebec.* Madison: University of Wisconsin Press, 1988.

Henderson, Stuart. "'While There Is Still Time ...': J. Murray Gibbon and the Spectacle of Difference in Three CPR Festivals, 1928–1931." *Journal of Canadian Studies/Revue d'études canadiennes* 39, no. 1 (Winter 2005): 139–74.

Jasen, Patricia. *Wild Things: Nature, Culture, and Tourism in Ontario, 1790–1914.* Toronto: University of Toronto Press, 1995.

Litt, Paul. "The Apotheosis of the Apothecary: Retailing and Consuming the Meaning of a Historic Site." *Journal of the Canadian Historical Association/Revue de la Société historique du Canada* 10 (1999): 297–322.

McKay, Ian. *The Quest of the Folk: Antimodernism and Cultural Selection in Twentieth-Century Nova Scotia.* Montreal: McGill-Queen's University Press, 1994.

McKay, Ian, and Robin Bates. *In the Province of History: The Making of the Public Past in Twentieth-Century Nova Scotia.* Montreal: McGill-Queen's University Press, 2010.

McRae, Matthew. "The Romance of Canada: Tourism and Nationalism Meet in Charlottetown, 1939." *Acadiensis* 34, no. 2 (Spring 2005): 26–45.

Morgan, Cecilia. *"A Happy Holiday": English-Canadians and Transatlantic Tourism, 1870–1930.* Toronto: University of Toronto Press, 2008.

Neatby, Nicole. "Meeting of Minds: North American Travel Writers and Government Tourist Publicity in Quebec, 1920–1955." *Histoire sociale/Social History* 36, no. 2 (November 2003): 465–95.

Noël, Françoise. "Old Home Week Celebrations as Tourism Promotion and Commemoration: North Bay, Ontario, 1925 and 1935." *Urban History Review* 37, no. 1 (Fall 2008): 36–47.

Osborne, Brian. "Moose Jaw's 'Great Escape': Constructing Tunnels, Deconstructing Heritage, Marketing Places." *Material History Review/Revue d'histoire de la culture matérielle* 55 (Spring 2002): 16–28.

Peers, Laura. "'Playing Ourselves': First Nations and Native American Interpreters at Living History Sites." *The Public Historian* 21, no. 4 (Fall 1999): 39–59.

Phillips, Ruth B. *Trading Identities: The Souvenir in Native North American Art from the Northeast, 1700–1900*. Montreal: McGill-Queen's University Press, 1998.

Raibmon, Paige. *Authentic Indians: Episodes of Encounter From the Late-Nineteenth-Century Northwest Coast*. Durham, NC: Duke University Press, 2005.

Rutherdale, Myra, and Jim Miller. "'It's Our Country': First Nations' Participation in the Indian Pavilion at Expo 67." *Journal of the Canadian Historical Association/Revue de la Société historique du Canada* 17, no. 2 (2006): 148–73.

Shaffer, Marguerite S. *See America First: Tourism and National Identity, 1880–1940*. Washington, DC: Smithsonian Institution Press, 2002.

Chapter Seven

Caritey, Christophe. "Manuels scolaires et mémoire historique au Québec: Questions de méthodes." *Histoire de l'éducation* 58 (May 1993): 137–64.

Clark, Penney. "Images of Aboriginal People in British Columbia Canadian History Textbooks." *Canadian Issues* (Fall 2006): 47–51.

Clark, Penney, and Yesman Post. "'A Natural Outcome of Free Schools': The Free Text-Book Branch in British Columbia 1908–1949." *Historical Studies in Education/Revue d'histoire de l'éducation* (December 2009): 23–45.

Coates, Colin M., and Cecilia Morgan. "Lessons in Loyalty: Children's Texts and Readers." Chap. 7 in *Heroines and History: Representations of Madeleine de Verchères and Laura Secord*. Toronto: University of Toronto Press, 2002.

Davis, Bob. *Whatever Happened to High-school History? Burying the Political Memory of our Youth, 1945–1995*. Toronto: J. Lorimer, 1995.

Friesen, Gerald, Del Muise, and David Northrup. "Variations on the Theme of Remembering: A National Survey of How Canadians

Use the Past." *Journal of the Canadian Historical Association/Revue de la Société historique du Canada* 20, no. 1 (2009): 221–48.

Igartua, José E. "The Genealogy of Stereotypes: French Canadians in Two English-Language Canadian History Textbooks." *Journal of Canadian Studies/Revue d'études canadians* 42, no. 3 (Fall 2008): 106–32.

– *The Other Quiet Revolution: National Identities in English Canada, 1945–1971.* Vancouver: University of British Columbia Press, 2006.

Lee, Peter, John Slater, Paddy Walsh, and John White. *The Aims of School History: The National Curriculum and Beyond.* With a preface by Denis Shemilt. London: The Institute of Education, University of London, 1992.

Létourneau, Jocelyn. *A History for the Future: Rewriting Memory and Identity in Quebec.* Translated by Phyllis Aronoff and Howard Scott. Montreal: McGill-Queen's University Press, 2004.

Nash, Gary B., Charlotte Crabtree, and Ross E. Dunn. *History on Trial: Culture Wars and the Teaching of the Past.* New York: Knopf, 1997.

Osborne, Ken. *In Defence of History: Teaching the Past and the Meaning of Democratic Citizenship.* Toronto: Our Schools Our Selves, 1995.

– "One Hundred Years of History Teaching in Manitoba Schools: Part 1: 1897–1927." *Manitoba History* 36 (Winter 1998): 3–25.

– "'Our History Syllabus Has Us Gasping': History in Canadian Schools – Past, Present, and Future." *Canadian Historical Review* 81, no. 3 (September 2000): 404–35.

– "Public Schooling and Citizenship in Canada." *Canadian Ethnic Studies/Études ethniques au Canada* 32, no. 1 (2000): 8–37.

– "Teaching History in the Schools: A Canadian Debate." *Journal of Curriculum Studies* 35, no. 5 (2003): 585–626.

Rosenzweig, Roy, and David Thelen. *The Presence of the Past: Popular Uses of History in American Life.* New York: Columbia University Press, 1998.

Sandwell, Ruth W., ed. *To the Past: History Education, Public Memory, and Citizenship in Canada.* Toronto: University of Toronto Press, 2006.

Seixas, Peter. "Teaching Working Class History in B.C." *Labour/Le Travail* 27 (Spring 1991): 195–9.

– ed. *Theorizing Historical Consciousness.* Toronto: University of Toronto Press, 2004.

Smith, Donald B. *Le Sauvage: The Native People in Quebec Historical Writing on the Heroic Period (1534–1663) of New France.* Ottawa: National Museums of Canada/Musées nationaux du Canada, 1974.

Stamp, Robert. *The Schools of Ontario, 1876–1976.* Toronto: University of Toronto Press, 1982.

von Heyking, Amy. *Creating Citizens: History and Identity in Alberta's Schools, 1905–1980.* Calgary: University of Alberta Press, 2006.

Wright, Donald. *The Professionalization of History in English Canada.* Toronto: University of Toronto Press, 2005.

Chapter Eight

Coombes, Annie E., ed. *Rethinking Settler Colonialism: History and Memory in Australia, Canada, Aotearoa New Zealand and South Africa.* Manchester: Manchester University Press, 2006.

Dick, Lyle. "A New History for a New Millennium: *Canada: A People's History.*" *Canadian Historical Review* 85, no. 1 (March 2004): 85–110.

Dickson-Gilmore, Jane E. "'This is My History, I Know Who I Am': History, Factionalist Competition, and the Assumption of Imposition in the Kahnawake Mohawk Nation." *Ethnohistory* 46, no. 3 (Summer 1999): 429–50.

Frank, David. "Minto 1932: The Origins and Significance of a New Brunswick Labour Landmark." *Acadiensis* 36, no. 2 (Spring 2007): 3–27.

Friesen, Gerald. *Citizens and Nations: An Essay on History, Communication, and Canada.* Toronto: University of Toronto Press, 2000.

Friesen, Joe. "'Canada: A People's History' as 'Journalists' History.'" *History Workshop Journal* 56, no. 1 (Autumn 2003): 184–203.

Gentile, Patrizia. "Capital Queers: Social Memory and Cold War Place(s) in Cold War Ottawa." In *Placing Memory and Remembering Place in Canada,* edited by James Opp and John C. Walsh,

187–214. Vancouver: University of British Columbia Press, 2010.

Heron, Craig. "The Labour Historian and Public History." *Labour/ Le Travail* 45 (Spring 2000): 171–97.

High, Steven. "Placing the Displaced Worker: Narrating Place in Deindustrializing Sturgeon Falls, Ontario." In *Placing Memory and Remembering Place in Canada*, edited by James Opp and John C. Walsh, 159–86. Vancouver: University of British Columbia Press, 2010.

Iacovetta, Franca, and Robert Ventresca. "Redress, Collective Memory, and the Politics of History." In *Enemies Within: Italians and Other Internees in Canada and Abroad*, edited by Angelo Principe, Roberto Perin, and Franca Iacovetta, 379–412. Toronto: University of Toronto Press, 2000.

McGowan, Mark. *Creating Canadian Historical Memory: The Case of the Famine Migration of 1847*. Ottawa: Canadian Historical Association, 2006.

McMahon, Colin. "Montreal's Ship Fever Monument: An Irish Famine Memorial in the Making." *The Canadian Journal of Irish Studies* 33, no. 1 (Spring 2007): 48–60.

Radforth, Ian. "Ethnic Minorities and Wartime Injustices: Redress Campaigns and Historical Narratives in Late-Twentieth-Century Canada." In *Settling and Unsettling Memories: Essays in Canadian Public History*, edited by Nicole Neatby and Peter Hodgins, 369–415. Toronto: University of Toronto Press, 2012.

Strong-Boag, Veronica. "Experts on Our Own Lives: Commemorating Canada at the Beginning of the 21st Century." *The Public Historian* 31, no. 1 (February 2009): 46–68.

Swyripa, Frances. "The Politics of Redress: The Contemporary Ukrainian-Canadian Campaign." In *Enemies Within: Italians and Other Internees in Canada and Abroad*, edited by Angelo Principe, Roberto Perin, and Franca Iacovetta, 357–78. Toronto: University of Toronto Press, 2000.

Index

Themes in Canadian History

Editors:
Colin Coates 2003–
Craig Heron 1997–2010
Franca Iacovetta 1997–1999